BRING OUT YOUR DEAD

BRING OUT

ELEGIES
FROM THE PLAGUE YEAR

YOUR DEAD

CHAD DAVIDSON

LOUISIANA STATE UNIVERSITY PRESS · BATON ROUGE

Published by Louisiana State University Press
lsupress.org

Copyright © 2024 by Chad Davidson
All rights reserved. Except in the case of brief quotations used in articles or reviews,
no part of this publication may be reproduced or transmitted in any format or by any
means without written permission of Louisiana State University Press.

LSU Press Paperback Original

DESIGNER: Barbara Neely Bourgoyne
TYPEFACE: Calluna

Cover illustration courtesy Unsplash/Chris Charles.

CATALOGING-IN-PUBLICATION DATA ARE AVAILABLE
FROM THE LIBRARY OF CONGRESS.

ISBN 978-0-8071-8126-3 (paperback)
ISBN 978-0-8071-8165-2 (epub)
ISBN 978-0-8071-8166-9 (pdf)

Contents

Acknowledgments

Grateful acknowledgment is made to the editors of the following journals, in which essays from this collection first appeared (though sometimes in different form): *Five Points:* "Like Normal People"; *Gettysburg Review:* "The Puzzle" and "Robot Coffee"; *Literary Matters:* "Homecoming"; *Ninth Letter:* "Unsent Letter to the Living #2."

"The Puzzle" was a Notable Essay in *Best American Essays 2022,* edited by Alexander Chee and Robert Atwan.

A fool's errand, obviously, to try and acknowledge everyone who helped in the production of this book. An errand it is, nonetheless, so let's. First off, this book is in memory of my father, whose ghost fills its pages. It is around him that the majority of these essays orbit, essays that try to capture a bit of his quiet, thoughtful, wry humor and—though I hardly ever heard him use the term—love. Not a day goes by I do not wish him back into this world, and so these essays, however inadequately, chart my various stages of grief.

To my sister Cyndee and brother Corey: strange to think we could have grown closer to one another through the tragedy of losing our father, which was a similar tragedy to losing our mother years prior. And yet I think it's true. We lean just a little more heavily on one another now, in this new, parentless kingdom. And lest you thought I forgot, I got you, Tamra Fry, Trenae Nelson, Marilyn Ocello, Sam and Lexi Melvin, and the Alligator (Clara Davidson). You're my tribe, and these essays aspire to form part of our linguistic totem.

For the actual writing, though—the nuts and bolts and showing up for work—I relied on the best group of writers I know: Dionne Irving Bremyer, whose rangy, imaginative suggestions for these essays inevitably made them stronger and much more expansive; Kevin Casper, who found humor where I had not initially intended and gravitas where I lacked it; Pam Murphy, whose careful, thoughtful, sensitive ear always tightened the prose and somehow (I know not how) rendered it all the more human; Sal Peralta, whose oversize heart found ways to make the essays just hurt more; and Josh Ferguson, who, on long runs on the weekends, would listen patiently to my latest struggles and always seem to offer a small bit of wisdom that unlocked a layer of complexity for me.

To Susannah Mintz, Greg Fraser, and John Poch: your friendship and constant companionship through this life is one more reason (and perhaps the best) I keep writing—to keep up with you! Micheal Crafton, Megan Sexton, Mark Drew, Ernest Suarez, Mike Mattison, Joe Oestreich, Matt Donovan, Aaron Bremyer, Lia Purpura, William Giraldi: your words and encouragement and belief in these essays do not go unnoticed. And, hey, Kate Sweeney: here's to another death book!

To all the wonderful folks at LSU Press—James Long, James Wilson, Sunny Rosen, Neal Novak, Alisa Plant, freelance editor Jo Ann Kiser, and so many others: a more professional, encouraging, supportive editorial team I could not imagine. It's a joy and privilege to work again with you.

For Gwen; none of this without you. And finally to my good friend Vince Verna, who appears in many of these essays and who knows me in ways I may not even recognize myself: this book is for you, brother.

BRING OUT YOUR DEAD

My Plague Year

"How is *despite* a preposition?" a student asked me.

The class was learning to diagram sentences: where the subject was, which type of verb, the necessary things. I was learning it all, too, sort of. I was doing a favor for the department in hard times.

My colleague who usually taught the course said early on that he would help when needed. "You will love that class," he had told me back in summer, and I believed him. "It's like seeing code." Besides, I *wanted* to teach, keep my mind busy, bury it in the minutiae of sentence patterns, parts of speech.

Despite functions as a preposition, I explained to the student, because it offers a relationship based on condition. "You can spot prepositions," I told her, "because they are almost always ancillary. Enhancements and cosmetics."

I had never taught that grammar class before, and I was teaching it online, which I had never done before, all during a pandemic. Lots of never-befores; lots of first times. Lots of virtual meetings, buffering and static, late-night drinking.

The student had to log out and back in. "Terrible connection, here," she said.

Her camera was off. She was just a voice somewhere.

"It's like code," I said, not wholly believing myself, so I gave her some examples:

"Despite my outward calm, I am increasingly anxious."

"Despite having been told by numerous people in positions of dubious and arbitrary power that everything is fine, I sometimes want to scream or punch something."

"Despite a creeping sense that none of it much matters, I continue to teach."

(Those are not the examples I gave her but rather *examples* of examples.)

Truth is that, despite knowing which form *despite* took in her example (preposition) and how it functioned (adverbially), truth is that it wasn't strictly code. *Despite* had become much more. It was not, as I told the student, ancillary, cosmetic. It was the way we were living. We were all living, despite everything else.

"Despite everything, everything continues." That's the example I should have given her.

"My plague year began with an ending" features a gerund ("ending"), which is a special kind of noun and also what my year began with. And, yes, I know full well that we are not supposed to end our sentences with prepositions. End them somehow we must, however, just as we begin anew, sentence after sentence.

Sentence can mean both a complete grammatical utterance as well as the length of a particular punishment. Both meanings apply here.

My plague year, though, *did* begin with an ending. In November of 2019, my father died, not wholly unexpected and yet. I had been planning, in fact, for years for the event, as had my brother and sister, all of us consciously staying closer to him, all the way back to my mother's death eight years before. Unlike a grammar class, however, we could not actually prepare for what awaited us in that new kingdom, as we washed ashore. Where were we? *When* were we, anyway, in that house full of our past together, the inscrutable jungle of our shared history, on the cusp of a pandemic?

In some ways, I could say that the plague provided an ideal backdrop for our grief, though surely that sounds perverse. Still, forced into isolation, we simply lived *externally* what we were already feeling *internally:* the world as living metaphor for sadness, for deep nostalgia, for pain and unease.

Early on I searched for manuals, how-to guides. I thought it might be useful to reread Camus's *The Plague*. I even bought it for my friend Vince. I said we should read it together, talk about it.

"Sounds like a plan," he said. "I definitely have the time."

The best parts of the Camus book, turns out, are the gory images of plagues past, which, in one early section, the character of Dr. Rieux inventories: "Athens, a charnel-house reeking to heaven and deserted even by the birds; Chinese towns cluttered up with victims silent in their agony; the convicts at Marseille piling rotting corpses into pits"; and so forth.

The problem, I quickly realized, was that I awoke to similar images in the news: workers in hazmat suits under a floodlight's glare; shirtless men digging furiously symmetrical graves somewhere in Brazil; funeral processions of somber people in masks and brightly colored scarves outside Mumbai; a crowded hospital loading-bay in New York, awash in the ghastly red of ambulance lights.

I finished the book, though I am not sure if Vince ever did. Truth is, apart from the gruesome stuff and piles of dead rats, the creepy descriptions of ganglia, the story was less interesting than I had remembered, and we mostly just let it drop from our periodic phone calls.

You can't read about a plague and be in one, too. At least you shouldn't. And carrying around the death of my father like another plague (a condition, a sentence), I had to ask myself what I was doing, reading about still other plagues. Weren't the current two—the pandemic, sure, but also the gnawing, persistent, deep, low grief for my father—weren't those plagues enough? Or was I headed toward some apocalyptic piling up of tragedy and menace, skies of blood and boiling seas?

Point is, you can't read about a plague and be in one, too. That's what I learned. We were living through at least a similar fear, a similar anxiety, a tenseness and electricity in the air.

"We were living through a pandemic."

There are ten basic sentence patterns in English. That's sentence pattern #6: subject + intransitive verb, where "we" is the subject and "were living" is the intransitive verb.

Those are the necessary parts, the important stuff.

☠

"Your gum line is receding," the dental hygienist told me through her face shield and mask. "You must be grinding your teeth at night." Much had already receded by then, of course: social life, a job with students around me, forays to the grocery store, stupid road trips, the sound of my father's voice. Much had receded, I thought, much more than the gum line on my upper-right molars.

Besides, isn't that what molars were *for*? to grind? What's the use of all this evolution if a thing conceived of and honed over millennia to serve as the ideal grinding instrument ultimately does me harm? The word *molar* even derives from the Latin *molaris,* meaning *millstone.* Much, though, was being ground down, much more than a few of my teeth.

But my class was not in etymology or evolutionary biology; and the hygienist in her mask—who busily scraped the inside of my bottom front teeth, where, she told me, the plaque buildup was typically worse—she was not my student.

"You should get a mouth guard," she said. "We make them here, form them to your mouth." She wiped bits of blood on the paper bib clipped around my neck.

Meanwhile I was busy foreseeing no end to the aggressively soft music piped into that white room, or to the slight edge on which my nerves set as I stepped into a business, any business—dentist office, plumbing shop, liquor store, gas station—and warily scanned my surroundings.

Warily. The grammar book for my class lists pairs of words often confused in English. *Lay* and *lie, break* and *brake,* and so forth. It doesn't mention *warily* and *wearily,* though it occurs to me that I have begun to scan my surroundings—begun to live, finally—using both adverbs.

Both A and B are correct.

☠

"Form and function" is what I kept telling my students. Take a simple, little word like *my,* a possessive pronoun: that's the *form* it takes: *my* receding gums, *my* existential death novel, *my* dead father, *my* rather pointless class on grammar.

Used in a sentence, however, placed in a particular context, that little word serves a specific grammatical *function.* For example: "The dental hygienist assessed my teeth." In that sentence, *my* functions as a determiner modifying *teeth,* which is in turn the object of the independent clause. All determiners are adjectives.

I have begun to dislike the word *determine,* which, etymologically speaking, means "to bring to termination, to end."

"It's very Saussurean," my grammarian colleague had told me, "very semiotic." We were kayaking one evening on the small lake my house abuts, right after the fall semester started. We were drinking a few beers, the sunset a slight rash over the spillway. Back then, the pandemic still felt a little surreal, an excuse to do little, to lounge around and read and fret, kayak in the evenings, drink too much. The most I could muster was a bit of strategy with my colleague regarding this class I had never taught.

"It's what I tell students," he said. "There is no essence in language."

It took me a few paddle strokes to catch up to his enthusiasm, almost nineteenth-century, almost Darwinian in its careful containment, its quiet awe for the majesty and resilience of any living thing.

"Words are not static," he said. "They change and morph."

A contrail tore at the pinkish sky.

"Language is a living thing."

So much dynamism, I thought, in his love of grammar, the ease with which he glided above the surface of any sentence on which I tested him, then calmly plunged into its particulars. So much dynamism, even as my life felt increasingly stuck, inert.

Words are not static, no, but that verb he used to describe them—that simple verb *are*—might just be the most static verb we have. It functions, I tell my students—like all forms of the verb *be*—as an *equal* sign, where the subject and what follows the verb are equal, reiterative, and, hence, static. A = B.

Thus "I am quietly scared."

Also "I am worried about things other than my teeth."

Also "I am nagged constantly by a low-level anxiety or misplaced grief or something else I cannot quite define."

Also "I am still here, despite."

That sentence is pattern #1.

Pattern #1 is, no surprise, the simplest, the most elemental.

My friend Vince, who works for the locomotive engineers' union in D.C., comes from a family of locomotive engineers (sentence pattern #6, again). His father lives in a trailer in northern Arizona. His mother is quietly losing her mind to dementia, somewhere in Tucson. (That's pattern #7, where "is losing" is the verb and "her mind" is the object, the thing presently being lost.)

My friend is in our nation's capital during a pandemic, trying to figure out how the hell to care for his mother, listen to his father's loneliness, keep his job, do right by his union brothers, and also not read Camus.

"It's a book best read when young," I said, trying to let him off the death-novel hook.

It occurs to me now that most things are best when young.

"Plus," I said, "we can't talk about a plague and live in another." He laughed a little, an uncomfortable laugh, like the one my hygienist used when I told her I loved the feel of the buffering wheel on my teeth.

"I *did* like the rats," Vince said.

Did, in that case, is an intensifier, but lots of things felt intense then, intense and yet strangely dull.

I remember when Vince drove trains, before he worked his way into union politics, or further back, when he was a lowly brakeman. I remember that he had to jump off in the middle of the high desert, scan underneath the wheels for rattlesnakes and copperheads. Inert things, dun-colored, coiled, and intense.

"Even with steel-toed boots," I remember Vince saying, "still some scary shit."

These days his job entails lobbying in Washington for his brothers of the tracks, while the railroad industry attempts to wring the workers for all they are worth, which, I suppose, is another kind of danger, another coiling.

In *Monty Python and the Holy Grail,* the scene Vince and I loved most as boys was the plague scene. The attendants of a rickshaw plod through the muck of a street, bodies stacked helter-skelter. "Bring out your dead!" one of them shouts. And people do: they bring out their dead, even their living. One man, in fact, pleads with the rickshaw workers—those collectors of corpses—to, please, take the person he's carrying on his back (father, grandfather, neighbor: the relationship is never formalized); that even if he's "not dead yet," he will be shortly.

"Please," says the man carrying the body, "do us a favor."

The dead stack up. They are threatening to overwhelm us. Inert things, dangerous things. Bring them out. Someone take them away. We cannot battle them.

"A constant battle," Vince says, too, about his job lobbying for his brothers, which is sort of how I feel about my class or, more precisely, how I feel about my *feelings* for my class, which is how I feel in turn about my feelings for my father, for I am needy and unprepared for the rigors of life after his death.

I am not battling big corporations or scanning for snakes. I am not a brother to anyone but my own siblings. I am, though, battling some version of myself who does not think that he will emerge from this pandemic the same as he was before.

"I will be somebody else": pattern #3.

For this "somebody else" I grind my teeth; for this "somebody else," I tried to glean strategy from Camus, even from Monty Python, tried to decipher the code.

I am a teacher of grammar, in other words, but a student of the plague. And I am struggling in class.

My class began to struggle, too. I was struggling to read their struggle. I had only "spoken" (via email or online chat) with a handful of them. "Reach out," I wrote constantly. (That's an imperative, pattern #6.) Sometimes, though, I felt as if I were simply talking to myself, which, when it came to struggle, I was.

Reassigned the course late in summer, I hastily Frankensteined a syllabus together with the help of my grammarian colleague. I posted assignments, constructed quizzes, kept my mind busy, tried to absorb more grammar, less alcohol.

After the semester began, the course-building largely complete, and with not many students reaching out, I found myself mostly alone in the weekly tutorials. I would set up shop in my home office, put on an actual button-down (not one of the four or five ratty t-shirts my wife, Gwen, had seriously begun to despise), and sit dutifully in front of my computer, listening to the silence.

I was hyperconscious of my teeth, my facial tension during those lonely sessions. I swore I saw the telltale swelling in my face mirrored on the computer screen. I hallucinated the grinding, the soreness deep in my jaw. A deep, bone pain. I kept threatening to get the mouth guard but never did. I sat in front of the computer for a few hours each week for nobody.

I thought of Camus's Dr. Rieux, who, despite the carnage, despite his inability to cure, despite everything, keeps showing up, doing his work, tending to those he has no hope of curing. It is what he chooses, what he *can* choose. But, really, what kind of choice is that?

I thought of Vince, thought of him back in the high desert, walking the line, looking for snakes. What was the proper analogy for that endless pandemic sameness, each day resembling the next? I holed up in the house, in sweats and a t-shirt, studying grammar for no particular purpose other than to be ready for students who never reached out because, let's face it, they were walking their own lines, in their own deserts.

Trains they could not (could not ever) control sat idle, desperate to start chugging along to wherever trains go.

Keep on keeping on. Drive that train, despite.

☠

I envy the breezy way Vince's coworkers and fellow engineers refer to him as "brother." "Thank you, brother," they write to him on social media, "for all the work you do on our behalf." And he returns the moniker, like an oath-sworn member of an antique guild. "You are welcome, brother." Monks and union members: a faint aura surrounds them both, surrounds Vince, too.

Vince is my oldest friend. We met in first grade and have been close pretty much ever since. The first photo I have of us is a team photo, a soccer team, The Sidewinders. My mother made the banner, on which a clumsy but lovable snake is busily digesting all the boys' names on the team. Vince and I are in the front row, on our knees. We are squinting and half-smiling. The snake is smiling, too, forked tongue dangling out, the California sun exquisite.

I thought of Vince's parents, how kind they always were to me. I thought of his mother's spacious Cadillac and her booming real-estate business; his father's long days working trains and his Silverado truck rumbling into the driveway at odd hours. I could not think of them as separate entities, estranged, deteriorating hundreds of miles from each other, thousands of miles from their son.

I thought of my friend thinking of them, and that distance felt even greater than the distance he used to drive trains, in a featureless desert west of Yuma.

He's like a brother to me, too, but not in that "Thank you, brother" way, more in that "I love you, brother" way, which we had recently begun saying to each other on a regular basis.

"I love you, brother" is an instance of apposition. Appositives rename or restate what come before them. For example: "Thank you, brother," where "brother" simply renames "you." They are the same. A = B.

Thus "My friend, the locomotive engineer . . ."

Also "Camus, the author of a ghastly book about the plague . . ."

Also "The writer of *this* ghastly book, a fearful person, given the circumstances . . ."

Lots of givens then, though we never once asked to be given them.

My students somehow started to improve, evolving maybe, or I wished that. They dutifully took their quizzes, performed admirably on the exams, began submitting their assignments on time. From the looks of my automated gradebook, I would have said that the indignant desert birds of Yeats's poem "The Second Coming"—his vision of the end of the world—were not reeling around us. I would have said that the charnel house of our country, wallowing in its own arrogant sense of superiority, finally had no ill effect on my students.

I would have said that, but I could not be sure. Behind their absence in the tutorial sessions, I sometimes hallucinated a grinding sound, true. I almost heard the evening sun grind down the edges of the poplars and pines outside my window. A metallic sound.

Truth is, my students were doing fine only in that most student of ways: the paper way, the performative way. Truth is, I wouldn't have recognized any of them if my life depended on it.

And I had become a little less recognizable, too, had lost weight precipitously starting in spring, which at first I welcomed. I was running obsessively, almost every morning, not eating as much, drinking more, my stomach often in knots, which I worried into telltale signs of sickness, disease, infection.

Truth is, catching myself in the mirror before leaving for the odd store run or plumbing supply, with my double mask and fogged-up glasses and beanie and scruff, truth is I hardly recognized myself.

Unrecognizable is also how Vince described his mother when she lost her mind, some sort of chemical switch every so often flipping, leaving the circuit open. She became paranoid, called the police for no reason, claimed that her son—my friend—had been in a terrible accident, which was never true.

We use the verb *trip* sometimes with electricity and so forth. "Tripping a breaker" means triggering a built-in shut-off mechanism. Nobody, however—not he or his sister or his brother—could see it coming, anticipate the trip.

In emails to my class, I talked about language change as rather sluggish. Language, I told them, tends not to want to change much and typically does so gradually, over long periods. When language does change rapidly, however, it does so not of its own organic tendencies but rather as a consequence of much larger social and political forces.

Extralinguistic factors, they're called: devastating wars, international shakeups, dissolution of the body politic.

I did not think that we were necessarily living through such an extralinguistic factor, one that could crumble the foundations of our language, create rifts and fissures of unanticipated proportions. In fact, the work of my class—the raw machinery—proceeded largely unaffected. The work served to reinforce the norms of our language.

Truth is, we can diagram fear and trembling just as easily as anything else. Maybe even *more* easily. Truth is, I found the work of diagramming sentences—during the pandemic, during my life washed out in grief—I found it all somewhat calming, if largely pointless.

I began to distrust the adverb *largely,* since all the work I did seemed selfish and small.

●

The worst part, Vince told me, was not knowing. "Nobody can see it coming," he said about his mother's turn toward that shadowy land of paranoia and fear, that Dantean hellscape. Nobody could anticipate just when or how that breaker would trip. Just as nobody could have really anticipated what sort of chaos would follow a virus that cares little for politics or geography or grammar or teeth or dead fathers.

I thought of Vince's parents, isolated from each other and from him, quietly going about their inert, fear-filled lives, all eerily predetermined, as if they were characters in a death novel.

I thought of my own parents and how amazing Vince was to me

when they died, my mother long ago, my father right before the plague. Vince was amazing in that unamazing, show-up-and-be-present way of old friends who can sit around in sweats after a shitty night of silence and sadness, and talk of nothing.

I wanted to return the favor—if that's the right word. I kept hallucinating the phone call when Vince would tell me that one or the other of his parents was gone. More than once I worked through the logistics necessary to attend the funeral, which would probably not have occurred anyway.

More than once I felt strangely grateful—if that's the right word—that my parents had not lived long enough to live through the plague.

"Intransitive verbs," I wrote to my students, "have no object, *cannot* have an object." For example: "Despite everything, everything continues," where *continues* functions as an intransitive verb, with no object.

This was unlike viruses, it seemed to me, which thrived on objects, possessed objects, had objectives, objectivized.

We were unwitting inductees into a Brotherhood of Random Genetic Mutation. We might have felt as if we had agency, that we ran the show, authored the text, drove the train, but—at least early in the pandemic— we were instead in some far-flung province with little or no ability to act, to make a difference, to alter course, and we possessed no means of transport out.

We were in the high desert. The rattling and the coiling.

"Thank you, brother," the virus seemed to say to us. "Thank you for all you do on my behalf."

For the virus, business was booming. It was all about transference. It was all about commerce and trade and the global marketplace and supply-chain optimization.

It was its own brotherhood, the virus, its own industry.

And we were the rails on which it rode.

Like Normal People

The autumn my father's cancer returned was not really autumn at all. Late September, 2018, and the ghastly globes of hydrangea withered and drooped in the heat. We could almost watch it all from our sunroom, an invisible force pulling the blossoms over, then down.

The diagnosis came after back pain had rendered my father nearly inert, almost bedridden. "He's literally crawling on the ground to get around," my sister had said the week before. She wanted me to call him, urge him to go to the hospital. "On the ground," she repeated.

That autumn, our cat went on a hunting spree, chipmunk after chipmunk dead on the kitchen floor, front porch, back deck. Others he brought in live, then let go. Gwen said that doing so combined two of our cat's favorite pastimes: hunting and doing nothing inside. When the scared thing scurried behind a dresser or under the washing machine, our cat waited a while, groomed a bit, then called it a day. We then had a live chipmunk in our house. "Your turn," Gwen said, a day or two before I called my father, as we pulled in the drive, and our cat loped into the garage, chipper in his maw.

The week before my father's diagnosis, when I called, he said the pain was terrible. Deep and dull. "Terrible," he said, which, if you had known my father, would seem remarkable, never one to complain about the body, even to speak of it, particularly its weaknesses. I told him he needed to go to the hospital. "What?" he said, the television too loud in the background, the cell-phone coverage spotty, all those waves bouncing off towers in the middle of north Texas.

He thought it was the same old sciatic nerve problem he had suffered through before, just normal (if terrible) pain. He said he was waiting to see if his doctor would prescribe him better painkillers, was waiting for a call, waiting it out.

My father was always waiting: waiting to take a trip to see his sister in California; waiting for me or my sister (on either coast) to visit him or for him to visit us; waiting for my brother, a half-hour away, to come for dinner, to bring his daughter down; waiting for the weather to turn, the rain to stop, the Cowboys to win; waiting to get over the loss of his cat Mikey earlier in the year, or my mother's death years ago, and to be okay with it. Waiting for the pain—in this case and many others—to go away.

"Don't *wait*," I said on the phone. He hemmed and hawed, something about his back feeling slightly better that day. "Don't *wait*," I repeated, but by then I was talking to myself. *Tell your father,* I said, *what he must do. Become the father here, you dolt.*

Instead I talked about a Peace Day celebration in my small town in Georgia, how a friend had asked if I would play drums for a big sing-along at the community center. "Why not," I said. "Sounds fun," my father said, and I pictured him reclining at an odd angle in his chair, three states away, positioning for a position with less pain, which is also what I was doing.

And that is how, with my father agonizing, not yet knowing the cause was cancer, with a cat we called Scourge of the Chipmunk, decimating the local fauna, I chatted with my father about drums, which is essentially nothing, which, under those conditions, I am very good at talking about.

That autumn was also the autumn of Vontae Davis, cornerback for the Buffalo Bills, who, in the middle of a game against the Chargers, simply quit and walked off the field. He told coaches and teammates earlier that he didn't feel like himself. "I'm done," he declared at halftime. Then he dressed into street clothes—probably an expensive suit, some designer shoes—and walked out. Coaches and fellow players seemed mostly surprised. "I never have seen that," linebacker Lorenzo Alexander said. "Pop Warner, high school, pros. Never heard of it. Never seen it."

I had never heard of the word *Junetember,* never seen it, though I recognized instantly what it meant when a friend complained of that unrelenting heat, that indefatigable August: no real autumn, just summer extended, the worst part of it anyway, the hot, wet stink of it. "Walking outside," he said, "it's like walking into a dog's mouth." Our air-conditioner kicked on even in the middle of the night with its high-pitched ring. Under those weeks, a low rumbling, an electrical static.

Gwen said I was crazy to ride my bike. I told her that I wouldn't be beaten by the weather, wouldn't let it dictate what I did. Besides, I thought, wouldn't it make me tougher, to acclimate, get used to it? In the gym, sometimes I see football players for the university wheezing through tight-fitting facemasks designed to restrict airflow, to accustom them to less oxygen, so that on game day their lungs soak in the rich air, and they become better versions of themselves. I told her all this, that we can get used to pain, that maybe we ought to. "Okay," she said, in a falsely cheery lilt, clearly signaling her complete disregard, "suit yourself."

When my father's PSA levels rose—which they discovered a week after I called, after I told him to go to the hospital, which he finally did and got the tests—I knew what it meant. The cancer had returned, the numbers said, and that was that. Originally in the prostate and radiated all to hell, obliterated, it had returned, metastasized in the bone. It's what the numbers stood for.

I love you, I said to my father in a dream that I wanted to think was a dream but which was just a wish. This was after the diagnosis. This was after the bike ride I was crazy to take, before the Peace Day celebration. I wanted to say that I loved him so much that I could overlook his stance on the environment and state's rights; that I could, if called upon, rip the cancer right out of him. What I really said, when the diagnosis came, was that we should wait to hear from the urologist, the radiologist, the oncologist: specialists, we call them. That we should gather all the data before forming a game plan.

I think I actually used the words *game plan,* which bothers me now.

Cycling in Georgia, in summer, is a kind of game, too. How long can I go and with what kind of supplies? How much water I bring takes into account distance, time of day, humidity, and my own stubborn sense of routine. "You're crazy," Gwen said, the day before I spoke with my father, before we knew it was cancer, as I strapped on my bike shoes. "Just go to the gym." She pointed to the ceiling fan above us. "Inside. Like normal people."

The sensible thing to do, for sure, and I found it difficult to explain to her my desire to bike outside in the hot, wet stink of that Georgia summer, especially one that had bled deep into September. I argued that we had just returned from a vacation with her family (true), and that a week of overeating, overdrinking merited this penance. The logic was flawed, I knew: I wanted to overexert because of overindulgence. I wanted to punish my body for my mind's bad decisions.

That autumn, after the family vacation, after the bike ride, after I had packed the drums in my small truck with the crooked bumper and pulled out of the garage, I noticed a small lump lying on the concrete between where the truck wheels had been. A chipmunk, dead maybe a day, ants busily assessing the work at hand, teaming up. Not wanting Gwen to come home and find it, I tried to flick the chipper on a dustpan but ended up just shuffling it across the garage floor, the ant crew perplexed but somehow focused, a black line following it all.

When I finally had that tiny body on the plastic scoop, I was struck by its weightlessness, how little it all cost, in the end, how little exertion it took to hoist such a complicated thing, with ants presently dismantling it, to place it inside a bag and dispose of it as one might the remains of a lunch.

"He didn't say nothing to nobody," Lorenzo Alexander said after Davis quit the Bills and walked out of his former life. "Just completely disrespectful."

How singular an event and yet how pedestrian, how utterly normal and every-day: the act of quitting, giving up. I do it all the time. Little quits and givings up. Professional football, though, is constructed of the uncommon, feeds on its own exceptionalism.

"I left everything the league wanted me to be," Davis later wrote, "playing for my teammates while injured, the gladiator mentality." I thought of that phrase *gladiator mentality*, itself a cancer, a growth that begins to eat away at its host. I watched our cat sit patiently with a chipmunk under his paws, under the heavy branches of the Bloodgood tree. I thought of how pedestrian dying is, too, how utterly mechanical in its systems. One swipe of a claw, one bite.

Gwen and I go back and forth on the topic. Are we heartless monsters, letting our pet ravage the chipmunk population? Or are we just normal people, respecting his instincts, his taut, eight-pound body a kind of miracle, shaped by domestication, by us, exquisitely designed for a single purpose, a perfect killer?

"Are you with the band?" people asked me, one after another, as I carried the drums around the community center's back wall, by the potluck tables and plastic forks and potato salad. This was after the bike ride, after the chipmunk dead in the garage. "Everybody, he's with the band."

People moved chairs out of the way, smiling their blank smiles of privilege and leisure, all the while fanning themselves with copies of the song lyrics. "Can you believe this heat?" someone said.

On stage, the musicians had gathered: an accomplished guitar player from town with his legs kicked up on a metal chair, noodling with the sound off; a bass player fussing with his amp, left arm resting on the instrument's neck slicked in sweat; a keyboardist who had a sideline catering events in town (muffins, artichoke dip, petit fours); and a djembe player named Hank, whom I instantly liked. Burly, bald, and jovial, his smile cut deep into his doughy cheeks. "I didn't make this one myself," he told me, pointing to his drum, "but I got two of my own at home."

The crowd milling about mostly comprised middle-aged women in yoga pants and sensible shoes: Danskos, Keens, Birkenstocks, and Chacos, all manner of Chacos: sports sandals with fabulously colored straps. "Rich hippies," Gwen often calls the women who wear them, the parking lot out front filled with their Subarus and Priuses. White women with sensible shoes and pension plans and the air of those who live the good life, who need not struggle, for whom a Peace Day celebration is a chance to celebrate openly their ability to celebrate, even in the pleasant burning down of a ridiculously hot afternoon (their only sacrifice).

The lyrics were hokey, of the *can't we all just get along* genus, the drumming—all the music, really—rudimentary and repetitive. Running through the tune a few times, I couldn't take my eyes off the footwear. Whatever else may have ailed these women, they would not—*could not*—suffer from sore feet. They would be damned if they'd tolerate sore feet. Life's just too short, too good, too normal, too insurable against risk.

That autumn, before the hokey Peace Day celebration with the caterer-keyboardist and jovial djembe player, before talking to my father, after Gwen said I was crazy, I took off on my bike. The route was an old standard, not too long, not too short. A few weeks since I had ridden seriously, a few pounds heavier from vacation, I turned a mile stretch along a traffic-heavy road into a time trial. Gearing down on the hill, I settled back in the saddle, dropped my hands to the curled bars, and dug in. Exhilarating, I thought, the wind in my face, a kind of hot wind, sticky and still rich with kudzu, as I passed a barn slowly being digested by the unstoppable vines.

I pushed hard for almost the entire mile, until my normal left turn approached, at which point I let off the pedals, rose to the top bars, and threw my arm out to signal. I had noticed the truck behind, slowing—it seemed at first—to wait for me. I coasted as I started my lean left (the same route I had ridden a hundred times), when that truck, traveling at least fifty miles per hour, passed me on the outside *left.*

Shock of wind. Smell of metal and friction. I came within inches of its passenger side, of the body of the truck, of dying on my road bike with the fancy red paint and carbon forks.

One of the chippers we discovered in the back bedroom after a couple of weeks, after my father's diagnosis, after Vontae Davis quit, after I nearly died on my fancy bike with carbon forks. Emaciated, the little thing's mouth was slightly open, teeth showing, eyes closed in a forceful way, pulled inward. Being torn to pieces, *rent,* in the biblical sense: even that seemed elevated, noble, compared to starving to death in a seldom used spare room, under the bed, next to Gwen's archival supplies.

I thought of James Dickey's poem "The Heaven of Animals," how he imagines their paradise as not devoid of danger and death but rather one in which those states are sanctified, made part of their animal desires. Not the angelic predator leaping from its perch in the tree onto the bright back of its prey; not when it tears the prey to pieces; but rather the prey's recognition that it *is* prey, that it is somehow fulfilling its spiritual rite, reinforcing its existence by being devoured.

It's their "reward," as Dickey puts it, "to walk under such trees in full knowledge of what is in glory above them." What's more, they feel "no fear, but acceptance, compliance." These soon-to-be-mauled will not—even in their own version of paradise—deviate from their calling. Heaven is a sundering, again and again, for eternity.

Hank accentuated each downbeat of my bass drum on his djembe. He smiled broadly, head tilted toward me, desperately synched, in touch with some untouchable—at least it seemed to me—spirit of world peace. That's what *djembe* means, anyway, though I doubt Hank knew it: *djé* from the Bambara verb for *gather; bé* from the noun for *peace.*

I want to think Vontae Davis experienced some moment of peace that day against the Chargers, that he looked up at the crowd and suddenly, perhaps (though I can't be sure, and I can't be sure of his own explanation), felt a calm overcome him, even in his tightly fitting pads designed to protect, inside that helmet, those cleats, all the gear it takes to play the game. "It all just popped," he said, "And when it popped, I just wanted to leave it all behind."

I do not believe in moments of transcendence, but I believe that others do. I believe in the elasticity of belief itself; that, like an electrical current, it can bend, and, by the power of our own minds, be bent itself. And though I more than once apologized to friends for my father's nerdy obsession with light bulbs and electrical currents, I did so as a cat lover does the scratches on his arms, as a father does the loving capriciousness of his son. Once, when friends from Italy visited his house and my father insisted on taking them on a tour of his "lab" (nothing more than a table in an upstairs room, replete with oscilloscopes, soldering irons, transistors, bins of vintage light bulbs), when they returned and I apologized, they said that I shouldn't, that they had enjoyed it. "Your dad," they said in the limited English they possessed, "he's calming." Odd how linguistic impoverishment often leads to richer sentiment.

I wish I could say the same for myself when I spoke with my father before the Peace Day celebration, after he had heard the news, that the pain was not the same old pain, the normal problem, but that it was cancer returned, a Lazarus.

It had returned, and so had I: returned to a boy, unable to make informed decisions; to talk to him about it all, how he felt, really felt; to say that I loved him. I bent the current of my language, redirected it toward a jumble of evasions and home-maintenance queries, talk of air filters, engine compression, and water lines, all the ways that pressure builds and can be dangerous.

Long before the diagnosis, before our cat (who is now six), before the sing-along, before the rest of my life, when the doctor originally told my father about the prostate cancer, about how treatable it was, how targeted the radiation would be, "a pinpoint strike," still my sister and I fretted. "Not this," we thought, "not now." Our mother had died a few years before that, complications after an ulcer surgery, sudden and unreal. "I can't deal with this," I remember my sister saying, "not now."

My father, however, was calm, said his doctor was confident of the treatment plan and of the cancer's responsiveness to it. "This won't be," the doctor told my father, "what finally kills you," a line my father repeated, like the tag to a film. I think he liked the sound of it, the absoluteness, the clearly defined limitations of the disease.

But did the doctor consider, I wonder now, the chances of its coming back, risen from the dead? Did his statement account for the ways in which a cancer travels, calling it quits in one place just to continue its work elsewhere? Isn't that what cancers do? Isn't that normal?

The music was hokey, yes, at the sing-along, yet the feel of falling into a tight rhythm—*a groove,* musicians call it—of letting go, felt somehow pleasant, as if I were carried along without effort, part of a current much larger than myself. That was, after all, the advertised aim of the event, the point: get a bunch of people together, stop talking, stop posturing, listen to the music, and sing.

"Great playing with you," Hank said, as I packed up my drums, "and don't worry about your dad. He'll be fine." The second part was a wish, which I read in Hank's broad smile, disarming and ebullient, excessive in its cheer. I imagined him saying that, because I wanted to hate his optimism, the optimism of that entire afternoon, that slightly conceited, if well intentioned, privileged, self-satisfied, sing-along afternoon. I wanted to hate the keyboardist-caterer. I wanted to hate all those rich, white women in sensible shoes. I wanted to hate the weather, the hot, wet stink of September.

And I wanted to rip the cancer out of my father with my bare hands like our cat does the life out of a chipper. I wanted Vontae Davis to suit up, get back in the lineup, damn it, violence begetting violence. What I did, though, was simply say my farewells to the other musicians, like normal people do, get in my truck with the crooked bumper and drums stacked in the back, and drive home.

On the way, I thought about my father agonizing. I tried to feel what he must have felt, but it was impossible. I tried to feel what Vontae Davis must have felt—not in quitting and walking off the field but rather in those moments in which he walked *on,* in full knowledge of what might happen to him, the incredible, theatrical, acrobatic violence implicit in a normal game of football.

I thought of our cat, too, whom I love more than I should, particularly given his behavior, which we can't help but think of as cruel, even though that gorgeous, eight-pound cat knows full well that it's his normal behavior, what he was designed to do.

I thought of the exquisite architecture of a cancer cell. "Your own body," a doctor friend once told me, "rebelling against you."

I thought and I thought until I entered what I can only call a calm, with the low hum of my tires on the asphalt meditational and soothing. I thought of the end of Dickey's poem, the climax, really—the point at which the prey is attacked, yes, ravaged, but simultaneously empowered, ennobled, made part of a great chain, a continuum.

"Fulfilling themselves without pain at the cycle's center," Dickey says, "they tremble, they walk under the tree, they fall, they are torn, they rise, they walk again."

Robot Coffee

"Ooh, robot coffee," Gwen said, as we passed by a squat, mocha-colored machine the size of a small car. People had gathered, curious about the pod-like structure plopped down in the Austin airport, outside the entrance to a new restaurant under construction. EXCUSE OUR PROGRESS, read the signs on plywood barriers.

Minutes before our flight and headed to the gate, we couldn't quite figure out how the system worked, how the coffee robot functioned. People huddled near its brightly lit screen, gleefully, we supposed, placing their digital orders. A placard close by said something about downloading the app. Maybe you paid online; maybe your credit card information was stored; maybe you just stuck a thumb on a sensor and the thing poured your favorite drink. Maybe the coffee robot intuited, learned. Like I said, we didn't get close enough to see the actual mechanism, but a line had formed. "Lookee there," I heard a woman say to her husband as they walked by the coffee robot, preposterously colored pillows, like gaskets, already secured around their necks. He chuckled.

We had just minutes before our flight, not because Gwen's mother had dallied. After our weekend visit, she had allowed plenty of time, even accounting for Monday-morning traffic. And though dense fog blanketed a low valley we had traversed east of the city, we made good time, until the GPS routed us strangely, circuitously. Maybe we missed a turn and the rerouting proved difficult. Maybe we momentarily lost our signal in that fog. In any case we ended up miles down a road seemingly headed nowhere, before Gwen's mother realized what we had done. At the terminal's curb, we hurried our goodbyes and hustled inside.

My mother-in-law is already halfway to robot coffee, having

switched years ago to the single-serving home machine, whose bright plastic cups fill the drawers of her kitchen, which is in turn a storehouse for the red Solo cups we drink from (writing our names on their sides with a Sharpie), paper napkins and all manner of plastic plates, bottled water everywhere, and not a drop from the tap to drink.

Heavy rains in Austin had, in fact, stirred up silt in Lake Travis that weekend, and the city had imposed a water ban. You either boiled it or bought it bottled, if you could find it at all. Up there, north of the city, however, in an isolated enclave named for the trees removed to build it, at my mother-in-law's house, the water was fine. We could have drunk it but mostly didn't. Instead we quickly became accustomed, reprogramming ourselves to reach for the cold, single-serving bottles in the fridge, for more and more of it in shrink-wrapped cases in the garage.

After we boarded the plane and settled into our seats, taking to our temporary oblivions (Gwen with her podcasts, me with music), still I couldn't stop thinking about robot coffee. Maybe it was Gwen's use of that nearly outdated word *robot*, a throwback to *The Jetsons* and its tin-can dream of the future. Or maybe the audacity of repackaging one of the oldest and most pedestrian forms of technology: the coffee machine. Maybe robot coffee was something else entirely, some evolved iteration, some heightened, tech-savvy delivery system, a caffeine-laced nepenthe for the over-traveled and weary.

In Book IV of *The Odyssey*, Helen laces the banquet wine with nepenthe, and everyone present—Odysseus's son Telemachus, Helen's cuckolded husband Menelaus, and, by extension, the specter of the entire Trojan War—falls into a deep, forgetful sleep in which grief and memory are erased. It's what *nepenthe* means: *no grief*. It's what Poe's narrator in "The Raven" asks for, too: some, as he puts it, "respite and nepenthe" from thinking of his beloved Lenore, dead and gone. "Quaff," he cries, "oh quaff this kind nepenthe and forget this lost Lenore!" Surely a great deal to ask of a coffee robot, but maybe I had. Had I, I thought, missed my chance at a grief-evacuating quaff?

My mother-in-law is already halfway to robot coffee, and I thought of her, alone in that new house not even a year, a house in which even the kitchen trash bin is automated: a sensor embedded in its lid; a winking, green light. She simply waves her hand above it, and the bin opens automatically.

"But it's *over*-automated," I said that weekend. "What if your hands are full of garbage? How do you wave?" She giggled, part amusement, part frustration. "I just like it," she said, waving her hand, waiting for the lid to rise before dumping a few spent coffee pods inside. "I don't have to touch anything."

It was 2018, then, and she had been alone in that new house not even a year, my father-in-law having died suddenly almost two years past, a heart attack. "I don't have to touch anything" is what she said.

On the plane, with my ambient music, I thought of Poe's narrator, alone in that chamber when the raven appears to him, comes to rest on the bust of Athena above the door. We all know the story. The poor guy imagines a talking raven as some emissary from the realm of the dead. He asks the bird a series of questions: *Where have you come from? What is your purpose? Are you benevolent or malevolent, friend or foe?*

He seeks to access the raven's knowledge, to learn of his own fate and that of his lost Lenore. I might even say he tries to *touch*, at least figuratively, the afterlife, Poe's melancholic scholar embodying the opposite of Gwen's mother, the opposite of robot coffee, too. Like a robot, however, and like the lid of my mother-in-law's kitchen trash bin (the hellmouth of that kitchen trash bin), automated and vacuous, the raven only dispenses rote information, repeats the simple word "Nevermore."

All weekend in Austin, there to see Gwen's mother, to see her new house, which was the same as the old house—same blindingly safe country-club neighborhood with fake, Italianesque street names and fake-ruined Roman columns by the entrance—all weekend with her mother, I obsessed over the hellmouth of her trash bin, mimicking its squeaky, motorized hinge, parroting its gadget-ness, its robot nature.

"My goodness," she said that Monday morning as we prepared to leave, "will I be happy when you're gone."

I was just kidding, I thought, just being silly. I felt bad that I had perhaps annoyed, even offended, her. I had even tried to oil the hinge, which did nothing to ease its low-level, barely audible, inoffensive—at least at first—ceaseless, repetitive grind.

Ghastly, grim, and ancient: somehow the hellmouth of that trash bin sounded to me thus, which is probably why I mocked it all weekend long, annoying my mother-in-law. Was it my frustration, or fear, or anxiety around my father's cancer? Was it that I used my robot miming as a primer, teaching myself how to utter death's name? Was it that I somehow asked my mother-in-law to recognize the trash bin as what it was, what it stood for, its hollow mouth just a grave-like welcome? It's how Poe's narrator refers to the raven as well: "ghastly, grim, and ancient Raven," he says, "wandering from the Nightly shore." It's what was missing, what was scrubbed clean in that immaculate house: reminders of grief.

When my father-in-law died suddenly two years prior, the family gathered in that same country-club enclave with the elegiac name, the same blindingly safe streets of manicured lawns and large, bronze stars pinned like ghastly specimens to the stone façades of houses. Brothers of my father-in-law huddled around the dark mahogany of the kitchen table to tell the old stories: how their brother had worked hard on the family farm, had been expected to; had once almost hanged his younger brother, had him balance on a tub with a rope around his neck, they said. It's what boys did, they said.

In *The Odyssey,* when the hero returns home disguised as a beggar, he must endure all manner of his friends and enemies (even his wife and son) talking about him as if he were dead. He hears (is forced, required to hear) what he should never hear: what others—particularly those closest to him—really think. In some ways, that's what the epic is most concerned with: what we leave behind.

After the service two years prior, my mother-in-law called me from the hallway of that house that was just like her new house, same hollowed-out space, an *open floorplan,* we call it, with little friction, little cordoning off.

"Follow me," she said, leading me into his bedroom closet. "Take as much as you want," she added, and waved a hand around his orderly things redolent of worn shoe leather and new carpet. "I'm getting rid of the rest." I dutifully chose a windbreaker and a few polos, a pair of periwinkle fur slippers, uneasy with the entire reclamation project. "It's how she processes grief," Gwen said later.

Robot coffee—any coffee, really—is a testament to the ease of savagery and darkness. Underpaid, exploited labor on majestic, savagely humid hills; roasted, desiccated beans ground into dust and consumed like the ashes of the dead.

There are cultures that do that openly. We do it quietly, darkly.

We have grown to adore the bitterness, the earthiness. We are both of the ground and above it, returning when we die. It's where the word *human* comes from. *Humus: those who bury their dead.* In this way, robot coffee—any coffee, really—is a *memento mori,* a stylized reminder of our own demise, a put-me-down masquerading as a pick-me-up.

That weekend in Austin, I took a run alongside the manicured fairways of the country club, a kind of Eden, a Gilead of the gleefully well off. Behind the wrought-iron fence and tasteful plantings of perennials, white-clad folks swatted at balls and buzzed around on their carts like crazed locusts, spritely lantana springing from rock-bordered roundabouts.

I thought of my father-in-law, how he had treated me to rounds of golf there, how he ribbed me lovingly, constantly, for my inconsistencies, and I him for his short, old-man shots, which were always straight. Father of three daughters, he had allowed my brothers-in-law and me somehow access to an inner life of his. I thought of how he would often talk nervously when we were together, repeating stories, until my mother-in-law would tap him lightly on the hand. "That's enough," she would say calmly, "they don't want to hear about that anymore."

But often enough we *did* want to hear. I remembered a story he told many times of having almost been drafted into the Vietnam War, how his father had called in a favor, how he was saved, led back to his life. I wondered if some part of him regretted it, even as the relief poured over him that day, poured like nepenthe. I thought of how he seemed always in the middle of a large book on military history, redrawing boundaries, imagining fire fights, machine-gun installations and bunkers dug into cliffs, all the ways we go on living dream lives, particularly when we don't know we're dreaming.

I remember his stories of Alaska, too, where he took his family (Gwen just three), where he worked on the pipeline, helped scratch oil from schist and pump it south to Valdez on night's Plutonian shore.

Had robot coffee offered me a portal to the afterlife, to a communion— however incongruous—with my father-in-law? And had I denied it?

Hermits of the seventeenth-century Saint-Paul-of-France order, also known as The Brothers of Death, used *memento mori* as their salutation. It's how they greeted each other. *Memento mori* is Latin for *Remember, you die;* Latin for that ghastly, grim, and ancient trash bin, automated, touchless as death itself. And though The Brothers of Death could not have possibly known the fabulous technologies we now enjoy, the trash bins, the robot coffee; though they could not have known, they probably did.

"What is your trash bin," I imagine them saying beneath their heavy, woolen hoods, "what is your robot coffee but simple metaphor?"

News, news of the world is what Telemachus sails forth from Ithaca to find. News of his father Odysseus, his undoing, perhaps even death. News of the underworld is what Poe's pallid scholar seeks from the raven, that "grim, ungainly, ghastly, gaunt, and ominous bird of yore." News whither his beloved has traveled, and where he too might one day tarry, and if this senseless suffering should persist for him and for his lost Lenore.

"Is there balm in Gilead," the folks around the robot coffee seemed to say, what the news from the newsstand called forth, in Austin's echoing terminal. Is there an end to our interminable tarrying? "Tempest tossed thee here ashore," Poe's wan worrier says to the bird, but he may as well have spoken straight into the mouth of my mother-in-law's trash bin.

I wear the windbreaker of my father-in-law in tempests foul and pissing rain. I wear it like a Brother of Death, hands clasped inside the vented, zippable, mesh-lined slits.

"That's enough," my mother-in-law would say, gently touching my father-in-law's hand, "they don't want to hear about that nevermore," or that was what I said of the crowd around the flittering screens of that mocha-colored machine the size of a small car in the Austin airport. "These people," I want to think that I thought, "just want nepenthe dressed in night's black anthem."

Just minutes before our flight, Gwen and I walked that soulless, high-ceilinged cathedral to transit, amid drab, featureless, suffering folks looking for abeyance, that there be balm in Gilead or West Palm Beach, or a Sandals resort on a nameless island with tiny umbrellas like shrouds atop coladas.

"That's enough," my mother-in-law almost said to me that Monday morning, "I don't want to hear about that anymore." She was tired of being tried, wanted only forgetfulness. And who the hell was I to say she didn't deserve her own neat, prim, quiet, vacuum-sealed nepenthe in a pod? "Will I be glad," she said, "when you are gone."

Gone four years now, my father-in-law, and I am pleased that we traveled, Gwen and I, back to Alaska years ago, a dream she'd harbored. Amazing what she remembered: the drive outside Fairbanks to a split-level squat above a country road, from which, winter mornings, her mother bundled her and her two sisters in down, and down the hill they went to wait for the bus in arctic black. Gwen took me right there, almost automatically, told me of the dog that had chased her as a kid; a big, black dog if not some terror sent from night's Plutonian shore, at least a pseudo-Cerberus of her own mind's making.

But I remember even more how we traveled to Childs Glacier, where the green-blue diaphanous wall, grim and ghastly, met the hellish brown, coffee-colored roiling mess of the Copper River. We gathered at its hellmouth to pay our deep respects to all the underworlds we fast ignore, this one reachable—like so many others—by ferry alone. The sky ashen, we sat on a table one might use for picnics, and waited, waited for the ways the earth gives way, falls apart. And when a car-sized chunk of that hoary glass snapped and slid under—not so much sinking as tearing apart in a reverse boil, a sudden chill into the brown-black winter water—it sent a wave across to us, who were safe on the far shore and of another world entirely.

And in my dream on that plane years later, after we had driven out of the fog-laden Austin valley, had made our way to our gate, had passed on robot coffee and settled in our airline seats bound for home; in that dream, my father-in-law walked over those waters of the Copper River—in the Chugach Mountains, by Childs Glacier—with the calm and privileged air of a god.

Duck

A stuffed duck, to be precise, which at first I thought was one of those big, chalky mushrooms that sprout intermittently here, the kind I take pleasure in running down as I mow the yard, plumes of white spores in the air. When a friend came over for a run and asked what that thing was in the yard, when I told him a mushroom, he took another look, scrutinizing it from the driveway.

"That's not a mushroom," he said, looking back at me with his head cocked. His car door was open, NPR playing in the background. Something about the wall on the Mexican border. "That's a duck."

A stuffed duck the size of a real duck, matted and sad, deep in our yard, away from the street, next to Gwen's small vegetable garden and a strange holly-like plant we don't really like, its dangerously pointed leaves and clusters of waxy, purple berries alien looking.

But what about this alien duck, this children's plaything suddenly manifest in our yard? Our neighbors in both directions, for houses and houses, are mostly older. We see very few kids. Could be a dog's chew toy, I reasoned quickly, brought here by our mischievous cat, whom we tragically misnamed after a state senator we both loved to hate.

History and experience was on my side, too, since our former cat had once brought back a red-and-white toy octopus, pranced onto the deck where Gwen and I were busy with some margaritas, celebrating our fair republic. (That was late in 2007.) The cat was so damn pleased with himself and his spoils, we couldn't help but see it as a sign that things would change, that good times, eight years' worth of good times— as prophesied in the lovable tentacles of that small, gangly octopus— would surely come.

For the dinosaurs, there was no duck, no ducking, no way out. Sixty-six million years ago, had I been there, and had I looked up, I would have seen a small but intensely bright light grow steadily in size (or, rather, *seem* to grow, as it neared Earth), until finally the asteroid's full dimensions— six miles wide by six miles long—carved a hole in the sky.

When it hit the earth, in the Yucatán Peninsula, at twenty thousand miles an hour (ten times the speed of a bullet); when it smashed into the crust of the planet with a force equal to 100 million megatons (100 million hydrogen bombs all at once); as this asteroid the size of Manhattan, the size of Mount Everest (take your pick), bore a crater sixty-two miles wide and nineteen miles deep; as it created a mega-tsunami 330 feet tall, which reached the shores of what are now Texas and Florida (where, thankfully, shallow gulf waters prevented the wave from reaching the height it would have in deeper waters, with estimates of almost three miles, *a three-mile-high wave*), it also sent massive amounts of super-heated dust and ash far into the atmosphere and beyond.

Some traces of this event have been detected on the Moon; bits of it even on Mars.

Was this duck a reprise of that octopus our cat had brought back all those years ago, our first cat, our dead cat? Was the duck a reiteration of that *previous* sign, that omen? Regardless of what it meant, what it might possibly mean (or maybe because of that), I couldn't bring myself to throw the duck away.

Gwen was repulsed by its mottled felt body.

"Gross," she said, as I held one of its orange feet, webbed and crunchy, between two fingers.

Not knowing what to do, I stowed it on top of a storage closet we keep in the garage (organic insecticides, recyclables, yard shoes, extension cords). Our cat often sleeps up there, on an old shower rug abandoned after we renovated the spare bathroom. If the cat brought that duck home, maybe he did it for a reason. Who was I, anyway, to muck with his system, erode his faith in me as one of the pride? I wanted to think that he might even (somehow) acknowledge the care I had taken with his toy, or playmate, or prey, or however we interpret the creatures of our creatures, that I had treated it with the respect it deserved.

A few days later, I was outside with Gwen while she watered the tomatoes. I was fussing with their cylindrical metal stays, which have always reminded me of those ever-widening gyres, massive funnel-shaped vortices in which falcons turn in the opening lines of Yeats's apocalyptic poem "The Second Coming."

"There's *another* one," I said to her as I walked behind the patch of Mexican Petunias marooned now in a sea of zoysia and centipede and bastard grass we let reclaim much of what the previous owners had labored to create there.

The closer I came, the less the thing looked like a mushroom, though, and more like a Nerf football or wad of yellow packing tape. This second toy deposited in our yard, turns out, was a Pluto. Not the mythical ruler of the underworld but the dopey Disney concoction, a stuffed pup with floppy head and paws, a flat body almost the precise size and shape of an ice-cube tray. Definitely a body meant to be chewed, a dog's toy.

The doctors, I thought. The doctors a few houses down had recently acquired a boisterous dervish of a poodle of some sort, along with an entirely new façade to their low-slung ranch house at the bend of the lake, where the willows genuflect, and a great oak spreads over their backyard and luxury camper. I had spotted our cat patrolling now and again their bit of shoreline, pestering the Canada geese, generally being an asshole. Could be, I reasoned, that he steals these toys from their yard—playthings of an ecstatic poodle—and brings them back, even though I had never seen any chew toys in that immaculate yard, by their immaculate boat, under their immaculate tree.

When I tossed the stuffed puppy toward our cat, however, he looked somewhat alarmed and sniffed it quizzically. I could see the soft tissue around his nostrils swell and retract. He didn't like it, recoiled a bit, as one does from the smell of spoiled milk. He didn't want anything to do with that thing, in fact, and slinked away low to the ground, throwing it a wary glance before darting into the monkey grass.

"There goes your doctor theory," Gwen said, her hose by then aimed at a sickly Serrano plant.

●

Was it a gift, an offering? Was it some compensation or consolation? an apology? some sign of foreboding and destruction? We didn't know, says Aeneas, didn't know what it meant or why the Greeks left it on our Trojan shores, that "horse of timber, tall as a hill," its ribs, he says in Virgil's *Aeneid,* "sheathed in planking of cut pine."

Some of his countrymen guess a god at play, that they would be daft not to show respect. "It should be hauled inside the walls," argues Thymoetes, and moored high on the citadel.

Others remain appreciably suspicious, ever wary of the Greeks.

"Into the sea with it," says Capys and his mates, "or burn it."

Laocoön proves most adamantly opposed, most vocal, and rails against his compatriots for their gullibility.

"A gift from the Danaans," he says, "and no ruse?" Are they nuts, finally, the Trojans, if they treat the horse as anything but trickery? He even suspects (and rightfully so) that Greek soldiers are at that very moment concealed in the belly of the thing. That or the horse is a battering ram or trebuchet, a way for Odysseus and company to pummel the Trojan citadel. Whatever it is, it's not a gift.

Then, in one of those small, Virgilian details of exacting verisimilitude, a bit of observation that makes the story—more than two thousand years later—seem lifelike and contemporary, Laocoön has had enough and hurls his spear at the horse.

"It stuck there trembling," Aeneas says, "and the rounded hull reverberated groaning at the blow."

Aeneas—all of the Trojans, really—should have known. He *knows* they should have known.

"If the gods had not worked against them, Aeneas reasons, he and his countrymen would have bloodied the thing with their steel. They would have ripped the horse apart, revealed it for what it was, and they would yet have their beloved city, "O Citadel of Priam towering still."

A sign misread, an empire sundered.

Navigating our neighborhood during those early days of Trump, 2017 or 2018 (I can't remember anymore, don't want to), I found it difficult not to read the billowing sails of American flags, all of them flapping over the porches and purposely distressed timbers of our neighbors' decks, as part of a ship having already left dock for some idealized land, everyone but us and our gaggle of university friends, it seemed, part of the crew, the in-crowd. Difficult not to read in the meticulously manicured lawns and fierceness of the homeowners' association various harbingers of impending doom. In timed releases throughout the year, sensibly colored signs for dangerous senators and commissioners (even coroners) rose from the ground, the force of it all like some deep, underground organism, chalky and white.

Or the way our asshole cat trotted into the house now and again with a chipmunk wriggling in his jaws: difficult not to pin his small, cruel exercises on a world seemingly tuned out of tolerance and goodwill.

"The best lack all conviction," writes Yeats in that same stormy, apocalyptic poem, "while the worst are full of passionate intensity." We are either good but lazy, or evil and empowered. Regardless, we're screwed.

Sometimes, though, the storms were real: flash flooding and freakish winds that whipped the lake into froth, toppled the wicker deck chairs and budget grill. Just as suddenly, though, the sky could calm itself, spread azure like cool linen across the waters, the trees relieved, a gauzy pink light fanning over us, and we could breathe again.

Those not incinerated, vaporized by the force of the asteroid's impact, or buried under debris as far away as modern New Jersey, could expect perhaps a worse fate. Traces, yes, of the dinosaur's cataclysm have been detected on the Moon and as far away as Mars. That dust and ash, though—90 percent of it, anyway, by then circling the entire planet—cooled in space and recondensed into tiny glass droplets the size of sand grains, which then fell back to Earth.

As they reentered, friction heated the atmosphere to incandescent temperatures. The surface of the planet broiled, the air turning red, temperatures soaring to 1200 degrees. Blood boiled in the bodies not just of the dinosaurs living in Central America or even in all the Americas. Rather *all* non-avian dinosaurs, everywhere on Earth, every last scaly one of them (and a host of other organisms) died within one day of the impact. Some scientists think it was a matter of hours.

The Cretaceous-Paleogene Extinction Event, we call it now, no more than a charred line deep in the sediment underneath us. And not one fossil of one single dinosaur has been found above it, anywhere on Earth.

A rock from space, a chance encounter, the end of an era.

We all know the story. The Trojans accept the horse as an offering. The Greek ships have not sailed away but instead lie concealed offshore at Tenedos, awaiting the sign. At night, the Greeks hidden in the horse's belly—Odysseus among them—exit and open the city gates. The ships return. That event, which signals the end of the Trojan empire, comprises an entire book of Virgil's *Aeneid,* some argue the best of the epic, the most Hollywood-like, anyway, with its violence and gore and fire and rubble.

Aeneas, one of the fortunate to have escaped, recounts it all later to Dido and her court at Carthage. At times he cries out in anguish, recalling the loss of his wife, Creusa, and of his friends, his city, all that he knew. But he also tells of a series of visitations and revelations, signs and omens, before the city fell. First, the ghost of Hector comes to

Aeneas in a dream. Hector is torn, his hair and beard matted and blood-ied, his corpse having been dragged behind the horse of Achilles.

"Give up and go," Hector counsels, "save yourself, out of these flames."

Still Aeneas hesitates. Even though he wakes to his city under siege—by then the fires are spreading, the howls of the fallen in the cool night air—even though the ghost of dead Hector gives him the out, still Aeneas wants to stand his ground and fight.

Next his immortal mother, Venus, appears as a waking vision, a hallucination, a haunting. In an eerie scene, she casts away the cloud through which no mortal can perceive of the work of the gods. Aeneas then beholds how it is Neptune who shakes the Trojan citadel to its foundation; how Juno, "raging in steel armor," holds the city gates; and, "look, turn," she motions to her son, "Pallas Tritonia couched in a stormcloud, lightening, with her Gorgon."

The signs are clear, she pretty much tells Aeneas: the citadel is lost; the gods are against you; find your father, your wife, your family, and flee.

☠

We were haunted, too, Gwen and I. Haunted by our dead cat, who still returned some nights as a pile of dark clothes in half light at the foot of the bed. We buried him, the two of us, in our yard under a rock by the lone beech tree, in 2015. Sometimes still, I find myself staring at the grave, when our pompous, lovable (but dickish) new cat appears; the cat whose dickish senator name sounds like our old cat's name, who looks somewhat like him—green eyes; short, black hair dusted in cinnamon—who (let's be honest) was supposed to *replace* our dead cat, *be* our dead cat.

And sometimes, when I am out there, monkeying around with him or tending to a potted plant, I pick him up and show him that grave. I tell him (a *cat*) that's where another cat is buried, one we loved very much and think of often. But the new cat squirms in my arms and just wants down to chase a butterfly or terrorize the cardinals foraging seed under the feeder.

The night he died, that first cat, a Russian plane went down. The charred fuselage—what was left of it anyway—smoldered on the television for hours, while I answered the vet's call, rushed to the hospital where our cat lay. It was smoldering when I left for the vet; it was smoldering when I returned with our dead cat wrapped and bound for eternity. It was smoldering in the crater it created.

Which was the sign? which the result of the other?

Aeneas finds his family in the chaos but does not initially lead them to safety. His mind is still bent on defense of home, on revenge and loyalty. Even after his wife begs him to, please, give up his lofty sense of civic duty and save them all, even then he just cannot quite play the family man, possessive still of a bit of that old, noble warrior's dream of a valiant death. Even the sight of his own son, Ascanius, whom Creusa holds up—his own offspring, his future—even that does little, we glean, to dampen his bloodlust.

"But then," Aeneas recounts, "a sudden portent came, a marvel."

As the parents stand watching, a point appears above the boy's head, "a tongue of flame," says Aeneas, "that touched but did not burn him, licking his fine hair, playing round his temples."

Understandably, Aeneas and Creusa do first what parents—what anyone—would do: they beat at the flaming hair, use water finally to extinguish the sacred fire. *Now that's a sign,* Aeneas seems to suggest. *Forget the ghosts and visitations from the dead. Give me a good old-fashioned burning orb atop my son's head, and I'll follow.*

But then Aeneas's father, Anchises, hesitates, calls for the gods to authenticate the event, requests a kind of corroborating miracle.

"Omnipotent Jupiter," he cries out, "grant us a new sign, and confirm this portent."

I find the whole thing rather rude, finally: requiring miracles to substantiate miracles, signs in service of other signs.

And yet the more I read the epic, the more I see it as a kind of primer on misinterpreting signs of all kinds. The Trojans, for all their valor and piousness, all their might and fancy dress, just seem rather incapable of reading the world around them. There they are, surrounded by their enemies, their city in flames, and Anchises has the nerve to ask the gods—whom they know are ultimately allowing this Greek trespass, overdetermining the entire extinction event—to attest to their own miraculous deed.

The gods, though, curiously comply, cooperate with Anchises's wish. Hardly has the old man finished asking when thunder rings out in the heavens. And if we were there with Aeneas and his family, on the ramparts of the besieged city of Troy on that sad day, we would have seen, too, what caused the thunder, what shook the very air around them.

"Out of the sky," says Aeneas, "through depths of night a star fell trailing flame and glided on, turning the night to day."

Finally the old man relents. And notwithstanding the fact that Creusa perishes during their flight, the men—three generations of Trojan blood: Anchises, the old man; Ascanius, the future of Troy; and Aeneas, our budding hero—escape the sacked city unscathed.

"Surely some revelation is at hand," writes Yeats. "Surely the Second Coming is at hand." And surely (finally), the Trojans heed the sign, read well the revelation. They understand, in other words, the meaning of the end.

And it only took a comet—a rock falling from the sky—to persuade them.

"You have any kids," folks asked us when we moved in eighteen years ago to this older development bordering a small lake. When we said, no, but that we had cats, they would look at us a bit funny, as if we had implied that it was none of their business. (It was not.) Two cats and no kids, we said, and they offered their fake smiles, signs of discontent or just discomfort, the kind of smiles that conceal smirks or something more barbed.

Didn't see that one coming, I imagined them thinking, wrapped in the warmth of their own assumptions. *Didn't see that one coming* is also sort of how the Trojans lose Troy: they could not see the trick behind the horse, the ruse behind the art. And the dinosaurs? Even if they saw it coming—that massive asteroid—even then, what's the difference?

Part of me liked it, too: disabusing our neighbors of at least some of that comfy idea of American bliss; the neat, chalky white community with kids kicking balls over fences, while an anxious dog slobbers on a toy in the shape of Chewbacca. Part of me enjoyed being the young university types with a no-sprinkler policy and dearth of jet skis, the push-mower and lithium-powered trimmers in the shed, the solar-powered lights.

Days of omens, harbingers, pestilence to come. The neighborhood just seemed changed, as if a veil had been drawn and we could see more clearly (and tragically) what lay right beside us all along. Or maybe I read too much into it all, into the guy who honked aggressively at me while I rode bikes with friends. I had edged outside of the bike lane, sure, but it was a seldom-used side road, no traffic in the other direction as far as he could see. No matter. He honked and yelled something incomprehensible, gunning his white cargo van around me.

And maybe I read too much into the fact that my dentist and all his staff are white in that white Antebellum mansion parceled out into examination rooms pumping '70s music—the kind of music most any white person can dig—while outside, as I awaited the porcelain crown on a back molar—a painting crew speaking Spanish got down to it, slung ladders over their shoulders, set up shop, and began scraping the old planks, taking the whole thing down to its timbers, all that whiteness littering the grass in a steady, midsummer snow.

Not until the third stuffed animal appeared, a few days later, across the street, in Margaret's yard—a stuffed bald eagle, wings akimbo and decked out in an American-flag shirt (another kind of sign)—did I convince myself that these toys were part of some larger pattern. They must be, I thought, more than simple playthings purloined by our stupid, show-off cat. Was someone sending us messages? Were these effigies of sorts? Were they signs we just weren't willing or able to decipher?

And then a monkey, under the limbs of our Japanese maple, the most prized of our trees, the so-called Crimson Queen, with its gnarled, Bonsai trunk and delicate, fern-like leaves. A flat monkey, another chew toy probably, but who was I to say? A week by then separated the sightings: four discrete stuffed animals (duck, puppy, eagle, monkey), the collection of these artifacts like fossils emerging from a dry riverbed.

Foxes, it came to me suddenly. It could be the foxes we had recently seen around the lake. Pulling into the driveway just days before the duck appeared, in fact, I had seen one sprint from the vegetable garden around the corner of the latticed deck, by the drooping hydrangea blossoms. And then another, crouched low to the ground by the Bloodgood maples, almost part of the earth itself, and right where I would later recover the Pluto toy.

I had spotted another a week or so before, as I was jogging by the soccer fields. Sleek and rust-colored—oversize ears and bushy tail— it darted by the empty goalposts and into a stand of pines. Another friend who lived close by had foxes take shelter in the culvert under his driveway a year or so prior. Some nights, their whines mixed with the wind, frightening everyone around. The foxes were out there, for sure, documented, attested to.

"Are you crazy," Gwen asked. "What's a fox want with a chew toy?"

She had a point. These fox sightings and stuffed-animal visitations— maybe they were coincidental, happenstance. With Virgil as my guide, however, with mounting tension in the political air, how was I to be sure?

Is the meaning in the sign or in us? Do we receive and interpret, or do we deliver and partake?

☻

The Aeneid, in some ways, teaches us how to *mis*read signs. Signs of doom, of end times, ultimately become signs of good fortune and destiny. The sack of Troy, at least in Virgil's telling, forces Aeneas and his people to flee, which provides for the founding of Rome. *Providing for,* providence, divine or otherwise: this is the other lesson of *The Aeneid.*

But that's our luxury as readers of the text: we know how it all turns out. Even Virgil began writing with the knowledge of where he wanted to end, with some mythic founding of the Caput Mundi, Rome herself, back-filled with Trojan heroism. And surely it was a bold move on Virgil's part: turning the Trojans—let's face it, losers—into the founders of the biggest empire the world had seen, at the apex of its influence. *The Aeneid,* finally, is an expression of state power and, thus, straight-up propaganda.

I'll be honest, too: I'm not quite sure if I'm inside another text now or steering this raft of a story over one; if I'm Trojanesque in my retro-misreading—now, during the plague year—of those stuffed animals as omens, or just willfully making much more of it than I should. But isn't that what the Trojans did, too? Made more out of that horse than they should?

Does that make my story one of providence or doom? Look at where we are now.

Part of me still wants to ask my neighbors, the doctors down the way, if the toys belonged to them, if their poodle's playthings had gone mysteriously missing. Just this morning, in fact, I heard the gruff, throaty barks of those foxes. (They are still around.)

Part of me half expects more toys to appear in the yard. If they do, though, does that confirm or deny my earlier reading of them as portents? Part of me wants to ask the doctors, yes, but part of me just wants to leave the whole episode a mystery. Part of me wants to see the foxes place a rhino or a bear or even a horse—a lovable, felt-skinned horse with wispy mane—down in the bastard grass beside the alien holly bush. Part of me does, but part of me does not.

I suppose that's what Aeneas thought, too, or how Virgil imagined him: indecisive, full of misgivings, prone to fear the worst. It's what makes Aeneas, in the end, so damn believable, lifelike, and fidgety. So doubtful, gloomy, and human.

Maybe that's the smaller lesson, too, of *The Aeneid:* not so much the Trojans' inability to read the signs but rather the universal human tendency to think of these things—thunder claps and bad dreams and whatnot—to think of these things not just as coincidence but as auguries, signs that point to other signs, especially when they don't.

"Out of the sky through depths of night a star fell trailing flame and glided on, turning the night to day": that could just as easily describe the asteroid that fell 66 million years ago and wiped the dinosaurs— surely the rulers of their realm—wiped them clean out. Unimaginable destruction and complete annihilation. *Near* complete, anyway. For what spelled doom for the dinosaurs ushered in the age of mammals, ultimately the age of us, with brains big enough to read the signs and read the signs that are *not* signs; to read, finally, *everything,* even the pollen caught in rock and deposited underground for 66 million years.

And when the interviewers on the podcast to which I was listening on my run—I couldn't bear to listen to actual news—when they asked the scientist, the one studying the asteroid impact, asked what we knew, if anything, of that day all those millions of years ago, when all those millions of dinosaurs simultaneously perished; if we knew, say, what time of year it was; when they asked, the scientist said that we knew with a fair degree of certainty that the day the dinosaurs all died, the day the asteroid descended "trailing flame" and ended the dinosaurs' reign on Earth just as a period can emphatically signal a sentence's closure and full stop; that that day must have been in June or July.

And when the interviewers asked how the scientist could possibly know that; how he could, with near absolute conviction, claim which season it was, almost to the month, when the asteroid fell, the scientist said because they had found in that rock and debris buried 66 million years ago, deposited in the ground and covered up like a burial or offering; that they had found pollen from two plants that only blossom during June and July, that they had found that pollen encased there, like a text to be read, which is what the scientists did.

That is why we know the day the dinosaurs died, the day after which everything was different, the day that began—that *provided for*—the slow, slow evolution of our own species, which would ultimately reign in the dinosaurs' place until who knows when, that day occurred sometime in June or July, a day much like this one here, on the shores of this small lake, a day between the flowering of the lotus and the flowering of the water lily.

Unsent Letter to the Living #1

Dear XXXXX,

It was late, both in the evening and in my father's life, when you visited us on your rounds. Late in the World Series, too, which glowed in the corner of that hospital room, the sound low, the stadium lights wild. My father slept or whatever passed for that. After shaking hands with me, you pulled a chair close to him and took his hand, coaxing him awake.

A batter was force-walked to first.

In hindsight, I should have noticed what all the doctors—the infectious disease expert, the palliative-care specialist with a fantastic coif and French last name, even the rotating guy they called *the hospitalist,* a term I had not previously heard, as if the ills of the structure, the building itself, required a particular professional—what they all were trying to tell us, in various idioms and workarounds: that my father's time had come, that we were five down in the bottom of the ninth.

It seems suddenly relevant that both a baseball game and Dante's *Inferno* are structured around the number nine.

I should have understood what you were all attempting: trying to prep us without having to give shape to words you knew we would not like. Such tending to, I know, takes time, relationships coaxed out of bedside chats and hand holding.

Take, for instance, the pitcher (any pitcher) in a game: if finally the point comes at which he must be pulled—86'ed, as the managers of a restaurant at which I worked as a kid said of the snapper some Friday nights—then he is first visited not just by the coach but by the entire in-field, those closest to him. He is convinced not just that he must leave, that his time is up, but that all of his team agrees. It is a communal resignation to fate, a group-induced *attaboy* in the form of individual pats on the butt, the back of the thigh.

All the touching, the tenderness.

By then the pitcher has conceded, has excised his hand from its glove, which now flops around, dangling like a lure from his fingers, as he sulks off to the underground. That I get.

What I don't get is everything else that led to that final meeting between us. You, his chief oncologist, the guy who had the final say in everything that went into his body, his dreams. In the six months prior, you became the sun around which my father's cancer orbited, the coach spitting seeds from the dugout as my father failed on the mound. Hit after hit after hit. You became, too, the garish stadium lights my family kept praying for. Just a problem with a breaker, we hoped, a faulty relay, and then, wham-o, let's play ball.

But let's first back up a year, when I visited my father, drove him to what we thought would be his last chemo session in your office. The room, nondescript, held rows of bulky, hospital-grade recliners, with large flat-screen televisions angled from the corners. A dull, fluorescent pallor prevailed, counterpoint to the photos pinned to heart-shaped construction paper on a wall by the toilets, and the sloganeering on nearby chalkboards and t-shirts and coffee mugs, declaring that so-and-so beat cancer or that what's-his-name kicked cancer's butt.

And though the fact that my father had a port surgically inserted into his chest and could literally be plugged in; though the assistants placed ice packs around his feet, asked him to grip ice packs with his hands—the cancer-fighting cocktail (a poison itself) proving especially hard on the fingers and toes, *extremities,* they're often called (though what wasn't extreme in those days?)—still amid the incessant beeps and chirps from rows of machines pumping chemicals through myriad tubes into living people, still my father remained in good spirits, hopeful of a winning season.

All around us slumped the beleaguered and disease-battered, those resigned to their losing records: an older woman, bandanna wrapped around her head, collapsing awkwardly over the side of her chair; a heavy-set man whose girth, whose inescapable presence on our plane of existence, was succumbing to the dueling toxicities of cancer and cure, the two of them duking it out in the arena of his capacious body.

"You've lost weight, haven't you," said an assistant as she flicked his IV line with a finger. Muffled coughs from the anteroom.

A cop show was on by then, one of those procedurals where smart-dressed, dour-faced detectives and perennially outraged district attorneys eat sandwiches over their cluttered desks, and always catch and convict the killer in the hour allotted to them. I could not follow what the killer had done, who he had killed.

My father was just as confused by the drama inside of him. He had not experienced much discomfort: no hair loss, no tin-tasting food or lack of sleep. Said he was a bit more tired than usual but that otherwise he felt great. "If I didn't know I was sick," he was fond of saying that spring, "I wouldn't know I was sick."

We chatted about our project for my weekend visit with him: to clean his workshop area in the garage. "So glad you're here," he said, as the IV beeped, indicating the bag had emptied into him, "I just can't do it on my own."

Thus on what we all believed was his last chemo session, I snapped a photo to share with my sister and brother. My father was recumbent, peering over his left shoulder, smiling, done. "Last day in the books," I wrote as a caption. "Dude's killing it."

Lots of lasts, during that last year of his life. Last time he visited us at our home in Georgia. Last time I visited him and cleaned his workshop, the third stall of his garage, which had become—over the years since my mother's death—increasingly freighted with the detritus of nostalgia and disrepair: languishing lawnmowers, severed extension cords, lampposts never installed, wobbly sawhorses, and a seldom-used, dangerously vintage, radial-arm saw inherited from his father. Last I saw of that saw, too.

But the first I saw of you, as you strode out of the back office, while my father finished the chemo, rubbed the tender spot on his chest where the nurse had just unplugged him. Yes, strode out in your Columbia vest, plaid work-shirt, and khakis: such strategic, unassuming dress for an oncologist who, I am pretty sure, drove the souped-up Corvette parked in the reserve spot, bottom tier of the parking garage.

Strode out as if floating, as if carried by the overwhelming esteem with which your staff revered you, my sentence there doubling back on itself the same way you peered at your reflection in my father's eyes, the way you looked back and forth, first at his left then his right eye. It was a peculiar manner of looking, which, when coupled with your tendency to talk over the ends of my father's sentences (as if to rush him along, coach him, *attaboy*), left me a bit, well, let us just say, unsatisfactorily satisfied.

On the backs of trucks, those HOW AM I DRIVING? stickers: do you ever wonder what the drivers think about how they themselves are driving? Or at least how they feel about a bumper sticker asking *us*? They do not wish for us to actually tell them how they're driving, unless they're driving wonderfully. Fittingly, when you were done cutting my father off, looking at yourself in his eyes, when you had turned back toward the door marked STAFF ONLY, I saw no such sticker on the back of your black, fleece-lined, Columbia vest.

No matter, I thought. It was my father's last day of chemo, maybe his last day of dealing with your walking over the ends of his sentences as a child might a scrap of bubble wrap. Besides we were headed to In-N-Out, his favorite burger chain, a holdover from our California past lately cropping up in Texas. We ate burgers and fries. We burned our tongues on those fiery, pickled peppers in the bin by the ketchup dispenser. We felt invincible. We felt grateful for each other. We outlined our afternoon chores on a thin, white napkin.

We know now, of course, that the entire thing was a sham: the World Series cast in doubt over a cheating scandal that involved the Astros' commandeering of camera footage, stealing the catcher's signals, which they relayed to the dugout, then to the batter through covert codes and taps on benches with bats. (Layers of obfuscation.) Just as I know now that my father's course of treatment was, at best, ineffective and, at worst, negligent.

Please understand: I do not blame you for my father's death. Just as I do not blame you for the Astros' disregard of protocol, of rules, of fair play. I do, however, blame you for the fact that we could not—my sister, brother, or I—ever reach you by phone during those harrowing final weeks of our father's life; or that, when you did appear, you did so unannounced, early in the morning, while he slept, or late in the evenings, while he slept.

And if we were there at all during those odd times, we were too tired or still asleep ourselves, too alone in our worry, worn down by the constant chirps of the leg-warming system, by the palliative care guy with the French last name and soft hands, who gently encouraged my father to give power of attorney to someone, anyone, and to give thought to whether he wished to be resuscitated. "Please," he repeated, gently rubbing my father's hands. "Give it some thought."

To be fair, though, there was too much giving for us to do: on forms, to nurses verbally. The information, the data, the anecdotes, the gratefulness. Not to mention all the giving my father had to do, in sacks and vials, in the hollowed-out holds needles feed. He rolled over for the nurses to change the sheets, for the doctors to examine this or that sadness.

Funny, how we had hoped for doctors to arrive and then, once they did, just wanted them to go away.

That you might go away again in your Corvette, under that expressionless sky thrown over those days like a damp sheet was all we could expect. That and the unassailable truth that your office staff, when we phoned, would cut us off, bark at us, tell us to wait our turn. "We have other patients, you know," one said to my sister, which of course we knew but could not understand. Just as we could not understand why your official assistant, whose name escapes me (as you did in your Corvette each night, as the cure from my father's wishes, from all our dreams), why she never returned our calls. Her voicemail became like unto the sound of death drifting over tragic Egypt.

And of your tragic Columbia vest and khakis, your notional attempt to *relate* to us through wardrobe alone: that merely contributed to your failure to understand the little we *did*—that our father was dying and that there was not much anyone could do. Which is why, when you insisted on talking about our father's "plumbing problems," dumbing down the metastatic prostate cancer and nephrostomy bags to bathroom analogies, I came to prefer (even long for) the heart-shaped construction paper and *attaboys.*

Our father was not a system, not a home-improvement project, not a weekend fix-it job calling for a guy named Junior in a beat-up F-150 with ladder racks welded onto its bed and—I swear, I have called on Junior many times—bins and bins of plastic and copper fittings, tubing and pipe, clamps, tape and (my personal favorite) escutcheons—little shields to hide a plumber's rough work on walls behind toilets and sinks.

I know because once I broke a pipe off behind our bathroom vanity, which my father and I fixed with a connecting piece called a Shark Bite. And when my father was wary of its hold, he said we should at least call in a certified plumber to sign off on our work, to sign off on it all. "I just don't trust myself," he said. "Not with that."

Always that care, that extra gesture of security, maddening to me when I was young and impatient; and now, since he is gone, maddening again, in a different way.

So we called Junior, my father and I, and Junior bent down by the vanity, said, "Looks good to me; would be the way I'd do it," charged us eighty dollars, and drove his F-150 out the drive. Last time I saw Junior, too. It's been years. He may be dead himself. Yet I remember him fondly as one who did the right thing, no bullshit, fixed only what needed to be fixed and charged no more. Showed up when called on. Did his job well. No hall-of-famer, but.

What I am trying to say is that I prefer the beat-up F-150 to the stupid, souped-up 'Vette.

Understand I'm not likening your job to that of a plumber. That's what *you* did. I'm actually doing the opposite, referring to Junior as a man possessed of appreciable amounts of tact and certitude and honesty. He didn't refer to our Shark Bite with condescension, didn't talk down our fix-it work. "Would be the way I'd do it," he simply said, and walked out eighty dollars the better for it but better in many ways, too, than you, who didn't show when needed, who condescended, who drove off not in an F-150 with ladder racks—a commitment to the craft, a sense that what carries one remains part of one's subtle significa-tion, that vehicles transport more than our physical bodies—but in a souped-up Corvette, a new one that looked like a cheap, plastic toy; that resembled a robot (and insensitive automaton) in the shape of an auto-mobile. Childish whimsy with a big block engine and $70,000 price tag.

That car, even its name—Corvette—once a sleek Spanish war ship, only later a car, an early attempt at an economy car, in fact (small, af-fordable, futuristic), and, later still, transformed into a hot rod simply by dropping a massive engine in it, retrofitting the thing to our desires, retooling for a market in need—it was the '50s, after all—of frivolous-ness masquerading as power, one of the first *muscle cars,* we call them.

Even that I would forgive you. Hell, my own father drove a '57 Chevy pretty much all his life, the second—and final—car he ever bought, which he did in 1960. (Why must I keep using that word *final?*) These days we replace cars as often as we replace toilets. *More* often, maybe, and with perhaps less care, less thoughtfulness. Not so, my father. That car embodied history, which he treated with respect, took care of, loved, at least in his mechanical, obsessive way.

A new Corvette, however, is a lifeless thing, a plastic thing, a sub-stance with no memory, like your office staff, your blank stare into my father's eyes, your crude, insensitive plumbing analogies to speak of my father's illness, as he battled cancer and we battled your people over the phone.

Maybe you care for too many patients. Maybe a distressingly ugly math is involved—when you know a patient has no hope, you simply fade away as might an aging pitcher, first pulled from weekly rotations, then posting up randomly in the bullpen, then finally, "Hey, whatever happened to what's-his-name," someone will say over a beer on a Friday night, the game in the background, "guy who pitched that no-hitter a few years back?"

This is not about baseball, though, or Corvettes. I don't want to stress the parallels too much, make more out of my analogies than would be sensitive. To tell you the truth, I don't even remember that much about the World Series. I remember the Astros in their frightfully bright outfits, the Nationals in their near-impossible run of wins to get there. I don't even like baseball that much, was watching it, as you might imagine, in order that I might not have to watch the other competitions: my father battling cancer, my family battling you.

A friend of mine tries always to turn me into a baseball fan, talks of all the subtleties, the art, the poise. "You *should* love it," he says, eyes full of wonder. The drama of the game, the way the coverage and commentary create little stories, narratives of struggle out of the looks on the individual players' faces. "It's like theater," he says, "or Homeric epic." He's fully given over to his pitch (no pun intended), selling me on baseball's enduring awesomeness. "The closest a sport can come to Greek tragedy."

Baseball just seems a lot of anxiety to me, a great deal of pressure on one person to make the right decision, always. In the heat of competition, that one fateful move can follow a player around for not just his career but for his entire life and beyond.

Do you understand what I am trying to say?

Do you remember that fateful home run by Kirk Gibson of the Los Angeles Dodgers, in the 1988 World Series? Hobbled by injuries to both legs, 86'ed from the starting lineup, Gibson was called to pinch hit in the bottom of the ninth, with two outs. He winced and limped bow-legged at each foul tip. It was painful even to watch. Seven minutes is a long time at bat. Gibson took seven minutes to foul and wait and wince and limp to that eighth pitch, which he put into the grandstands for a walk-off home run. Good night, Junior.

That's back when we lived in California, when I tried, for my grand-father's sake, to be a Dodgers fan, and *was,* for a short run. But who could ever outdo that magical moment in baseball history for me? Like I said, I'm not much for the game anymore, particularly after I watched it while my father suffered in a bed not three feet from the unreal green of that idealized field on television. And like I said, too, I don't remember much about the series. I can't even tell you—honestly cannot tell you and will not look it up, do not *want* to look it up—who even won. I don't even know who won the World Series, the one that will forever be linked in my mind to my father's death.

I do not—I swear on my father's '57 Chevy, sea-foam green and with me still—I do not know who won. Only who lost.

Sincerely,
Chad

Jupiter

"There's the turn," Ben said, his voice trending giddily upward. "Wait until you see this place."

We pulled onto a gravel road leading to a whitewashed farmhouse, a few cars nosed into its façade. A formidable dark, oily and totalizing, had descended. Not far from Fort William, in the southwest corner of the Scottish Highlands, but we could have been anywhere at that point, since the inn seemed detached from geography, suspended between dark ground (wet, always wet and spongy) and a matte-finish sky in which no cloud, no moonlight, no tree tousling in the wind assured us of any world beyond. We lugged the suitcases into the low-ceilinged hallway, the yellow lamplight heavy, the framed photos on the wall excessively vintage. A shaggy dog lay near the fireplace, or I may simply want to remember it that way.

There to visit my friend and the country my grandfather came from, all of us—my parents, my aunt, Gwen and I—were never more content than when we could dump our bags in rooms and gather in the bar. This one, at the Kingshouse Inn, was all dark wood paneling and a light I can only perceive of now, at this remove (some twenty years past), as ancient, the kind given off by torches, imperial edicts, dying stars; a light with volume and mass.

And we had readily learned to anticipate our pint and whisky each night, my father and Gwen gravitating toward the astringent, peaty, single malts, which tasted to me of flannel and austerity. Ben and I pre-ferred the richer varieties, sherry colored, their pigments pulled from cask wood, flavors caramelized and residual, with a heady, turpentine viscosity. My aunt passed on the whisky and instead just nursed her pint. I think my mother asked for Diet Coke.

We had grown accustomed, too, to dense meals of meat, of root vegetables pried, it seemed, out of that unforgiving, rocky soil and interminable damp; to the muted, almost tin-like northern light. Just four days into our trip, but we had also grown used to traveling with each other, our idiosyncrasies and competing desires, all of which were easily mollified, massaged into community with some strong, dark beer, a dram of whisky, a warm fire, and a night's sleep. When we finally called it quits and retired to our rooms—strangely midcentury furnishings, shag rugs in groovy colors (burnt orange, avocado green)—Gwen and I felt pleasantly of that place, like bunking over at a grandparent's house.

Yet when I woke the next morning, after a few hours of half listening to the windows flex in the wind, to what sounded like (what in fact *was*) sleet blasting the glass at intervals; when I walked to the thick curtains, which smelled of cigarettes and dust, and pulled them back, I beheld a vast plain of muted, brittle, yellow-orange grass, out of which erupted knobby rocks, like warts, with the monolith of Buachaille Etive Mòr, rising humpbacked and ominous, almost framed by the window, otherworldly in that treeless, doleful expanse.

We had landed in foreign terrain, yes, but almost *beyond* foreign: unnamable, untraceable. With the sleet blowing nearly sideways, the effect was one of static on an old television console or a monitor in some mock sci-fi control room. The effect was anachronistic, like the carpet and low-back contemporary chairs, the wainscoting and lamps. Because we had arrived in the Highlands the night before in that seemingly impenetrable nothingness, that void of space and time, I felt suddenly transported as I opened those curtains, as if I were staring out the portal of a retro-style spaceship at a new, uncharted realm.

In August 2011, NASA launched the Juno probe, whose principal goal, in their words, is to "understand the origin and evolution of Jupiter."

The craft took the better part of five years to make its journey, arriving at the gas giant in the summer (*our* summer, Earth's summer) of 2016. Engineers used our own planet's orbit to slingshot the probe into deep, dark distances: fantastic feats of mathematics and physics, timing and patience.

We talked about Juno—my father, Gwen, and I—when he visited us for what (we could not have known then) was the last time, three years ago. An enthusiast of space travel and all things science-related, he followed all the latest NASA projects with boyish zeal. We sat in our living room, in low-back chairs strangely similar to those in that Highlands inn, time repeating itself.

We rehashed that Scotland trip, too, as we always did. "A 'wee dram,' remember?" my father said, when Gwen brought some bourbon in tumblers. Not whisky, no, by Scottish definition, but still recalling for him our nights together in musty pubs and farmhouses, sipping our pints and spirits.

And of course I remembered it all. I remembered and called forth the same things we always talked about when we talked about that trip: how I once (just once) pulled onto a two-lane country highway, onto the wrong side, and drove for a while before Gwen realized; how we ate haggis any chance we could get (Ben, an English transplant living outside Glasgow, knew all the choice venues); how my father snapped a photo of Ben and me at Loch Ness, the two of us astride a hapless representation of Nessie herself in molded plastic; how, once, at a place called The Drovers Inn, we drank pints in a cramped, smoky, hut-like structure, while geese patrolled the front door landing, and a horse (an actual, non-molded-plastic horse) walked in.

We talked about everything but the void at the center of the story: my mother gone, dead eight years by then. And, yes, twenty years have passed now since that Highlands trip, the last third or so of which my father lived alone, until his death. In fact he had taken to inhabiting more and more that previous realm, retreating into the darkened interiors of a former life. Part of it, no doubt—that tendency to dwell in the past—must have been in response to his ailing body. He could no longer do much of anything active, things that once suited him well, meditational things: jogging, hiking, gardening, even just walking a pet late after dinner, down his dimly lit street. He became less and less sure on his feet those final years, his knees having given way, succumbing to gravity and the disintegrating tendencies of tendons and age itself.

During that last visit he made, we lit a fire down by the lake not fifty yards from our house. Negotiating the uneven ground, he fell on his way back. I saw it but didn't say anything, instead just waited for him to slowly prop himself up (praying he could do it, that he hadn't broken a hip), and acted like all was fine, relieved but shocked at his frailness.

Part of his receding into the past, though, seemed like travel to another world, another sphere of being. He recalled things my mother and he did together with a kind of meticulous, almost scientific specificity, as if detailing life on a distant planet. "No," he'd correct me on some fact, as he rocked back and forth in his chair, hands nervously rubbing his knees, "must have been '94, right after we moved."

That place—whatever year or former world he revisited—remained verdant, crowded with living things, hyper-oxygenated; a place where everyone seemed expectant, optimistic, and swell. The mail and trains arrived on time; the exacting grandfather clock in the seldom-used living room of my parents' house chimed not so much as ominous reminder but rather as joyous renewal; pets, long dead, were resurrected; friends, long gone, reanimated; the Christmas cactus in the foyer perennially shot through with its hanging, purple-white, prawn-shaped blossoms.

"Underneath its dense cloud cover," the NASA literature continues, "Jupiter safeguards secrets to the fundamental processes and conditions that governed our solar system during its formation." Jupiter, in other words, might tell us more about where Earth, where the Sun, where the whole mess of planets and rocks we float in: where it all, including us, came from. Jupiter, after all, takes its name from the father of gods: *Deus Pater.*

We had planned the Scotland trip for many reasons. Gwen and I would be in Italy that entire year and knew my parents would make the trek. They had always wanted to visit Scotland, so why not tack on a side excursion? My father's father was an obsessive booster, having been born outside Glasgow and emigrated as a boy. Above his fireplace, he had painted a Scottish saying, which we grandkids always asked him to recite, and which he loved to do: *Gin yer hert be cauld, a canna warm ye.* He'd smile wide, reclining in his leather rocker, in thick-rimmed glasses, in front of the country-themed wallpaper. To us—my sister, brother, and I, as well as our two cousins—that folksy wisdom seemed some relic of a foreign language, and Scotland may as well have been another planet, unknowable, a remnant or fossil, that enigmatic quote from a past we had no inkling of.

We had planned the trip, too, because my uncle had died a few years before that. My aunt was cleaving a bit more tightly to my father (her brother), or we at least welcomed the renewed closeness. A trip for all of us would strengthen those bonds. And with my good friend Ben living at the time just outside Glasgow, working for an IBM call center, the timing was ideal.

When I asked him where he lived in relation to where my father's family was buried, he repeated the town name to me quizzically.

"Helensburgh? Are you serious?" he said. "That's right across the water from me."

Amazing coincidences, small spheres of relationships colliding in unfathomably large systems. We booked our tickets that same day.

As I write this, Juno remains in a highly elliptical orbit around Jupiter. The probe comes within 2,100 miles of the planet's cloud tops (a layer thirty miles thick) before being hurled 5 million miles away, at speeds of over 1,800 feet per second. Every fifty-three days, the probe makes another pass around the polar region of the gas giant and streams back data and images, photos unreal in their captivating beauty and strangeness. Since Jupiter was the first of our system's planets to form out of the cosmic explosion, looking at these images now is like peering into the distant past.

That past my father shared with my mother possessed an enormous hold on him in those late years. He was drawn, pulled unwittingly into its gravity: the closet in his bedroom heavy with her clothing; attic boxes full of Christmas decorations, all my mother's gatherings of things, collections upon collections. Obsessive but also mercurial in her tastes, she left my father a shadowy world of trunks and bins, scraps and shards.

One of her favorite collections was Snow Village: ceramic models of main-street shops and gingerbread houses all corbeled and sentimentally etched in snow. She displayed the growing set each December as a kind of diorama, a small town floating on its white-cotton, glitter-speckled base; an old mirror serving as a frozen lake on which Snow Village denizens (you could buy figurines, too) carved their infinity signs.

Originally occupying an end table, the whole thing quickly outgrew its boundaries and rezoned itself, colonizing the piano top and, by the end, the last decade or so my mother worked on it, commanding the floor around an entire Christmas tree, a *second* one (synthetic, unlike their primary tree), encircled by my father's old model train. The place was a functioning colony, a community unto itself, with a transit system, suburban sprawl, even a modest entertainment district (movie theater, ice cream shop, etc.).

I may have been asked if I wanted some of the collection after my mother died, but I can't remember now. Not much on collecting, Gwen and I mostly just end up feeling callous and stony when we sheepishly decline offers from family members of china, heirloom platters, tchotchkes, and trinkets. I have, however, become more sentimental, at least in my own way. The times my father came to visit, I pampered him the way a grandparent might spoil a first grandchild. With no kids ourselves, Gwen and I readily fussed over him, planned dinners, invited friends, took him shopping, dressed him up.

That night during his last visit, before Gwen brought us the bourbon, I had dusted off a model crane he built for me years ago out of PVC pipe and a barbeque-spit motor. The whole thing runs on rubber-band pulleys. I challenged him, as I always did, to little competitions, each more absurd than the last. We graduated quickly from dropping nails in small bowls, to balancing tiny washers on the tops of floor-lamp plugs, threading long screws into the perforations of a small erector-set girder, which formed part of the crane's first iteration, built by my father when he was a boy.

He had difficulty with the final challenge: trying to open the plastic lid of my toolbox with the crane's magnetized head and then depositing a screw inside a small, inset bin. He swung the base around too quickly, not paying attention to the speed, sending the magnet—like the lag on a trebuchet—even harder into a nearby plant stand.

"Ooh," I said with a mock cringe, "twelve die in freakish crane accident. Operator believed drunk."

He smiled and handed me the controls, then sipped his bourbon.

Part of my bringing the crane out, though, part of all the pampering we showed him, had to do with our growing inevitably apart, with fewer and fewer commonalities. In Texas, among his particular group of friends, he had become increasingly and more stridently conservative, a fact that made conversation with him difficult on most any topic but home improvement, and sometimes not even that. It's as if the air he breathed in that house, in that north Texas enclave—farmland when my parents moved there but, later, fabulously wealthy on an over-charged economy—it's as if the air itself were different, an alien and alienating atmosphere promoting conspiracies and fears of otherness.

Loving a parent who's both declining and lonely but also frustratingly polarizing: this was a particular kind of conundrum. We were like different species no longer compatible, two planets in ever-divergent orbits.

Images taken by the Juno probe present Jupiter in all its eerie specificity, with vivid red auroras and a South Pole awash in swirling blues like those in the childlike night sky of van Gogh's *The Starry Night*. It's that beautiful, that seemingly innocent, lovingly framed and probably color-enhanced by scientists (maybe artists, too) somewhere in a nondescript building, in Houston or Pasadena. Cyclones and anticyclones, some half the size of Earth; what the website refers to as "atmospheric conditions," which resemble grand, abstract sand-sculptures, or the whimsy of oil floating on water.

And then, of course, the resplendent Great Red Spot: a storm of incredible magnitude (the largest known vortex in our galaxy), consistently observed since 1830. Mentions of a massive blemish on Jupiter, perhaps this same anticyclonic disturbance, are attested to as early as the 1600s.

There is a Jovian storm, in other words, that is older than our country, larger than our planet, beautiful and unfathomable. Beautiful *because* unfathomable.

You can watch all of this—the orb spinning its bands of storms, the Great Red Spot included, in opposing directions—on NASA's website.

Rings of storms, like rivers of muted, pastel mica.

If we were not playing with the crane, my father and I were involved in small home-improvement tasks. *Projects,* we called them, a list of which I compiled for his visits: a table lamp, maybe, in need of a new socket seat; a wobbly ceiling fan; some fuse-box issues and light-duty paint jobs. Half the list was composed of things I could have tended to on my own but hadn't; the other half I pretty much invented. We communicated through the completion of them, the simple pleasure of ticking tasks off a list. It was the closest we could come, probably, to declaring openly our feelings for one another.

At night, after dinner and bourbon, we would watch Nova episodes and Science Channel documentaries, and pause the video whenever my father wanted to add more to the discussion, what he had read in magazines. No expert, still he possessed a keen interest in (and incredible memory for) all the minutiae of space and what's out there. "Venus has lakes, too," he told me once, as we stared out onto our little lake, "only they're made of liquid metal."

He exhibited a kind of childlike enthusiasm and wonder, and, really,

I was amazed as well. "Over 200 billion stars in our own galaxy," he told me that week of his last visit, "and over 200 billion galaxies just like ours." The sheer size harrows, intimidates, yes, but also astounds.

10 to the 22nd sounds less frightening as a number. That's how many planets we assume are out there, spinning around their stars, most of which would dwarf our tiny, otherwise inconsequential Sun.

❈

Jupiter's atmosphere is a curious thing, nearly solar in its proportions of helium and hydrogen. With methane and consistent lightning strikes, soot would fall from the Jovian skies. As it descended through the various atmospheric levels (troposphere, stratosphere, thermosphere, exosphere), the pressure on that falling carbon could potentially create graphite and, finally, something even harder. On Jupiter—as on other gas giants—it could literally rain diamonds.

"Diamonds," my father said, barely able to conceal the awe. And I have to admit that the idea thrilled me, too. I am still repeating it to friends: Earth-sized storms raining gems. It's like that scene in *Candide*, when the weary, European travelers encounter a South American tribe whose gold stores are immense but who treat it like simple rock: common and worthless. The image in my mind—rain made of diamonds—even as normal rain falls outside my windows on this small lake here at home, the stippling effect on the water—is exhilarating.

Mostly, though, I found those galactic possibilities depressing. Even as our lay knowledge of the universe and its magnitude increased, my father was nearing the end of his own galaxy. "When you were born," he liked to say a few years ago, "I was almost thirty times your age." He would then crack his smug smile. "Now, I am not even *twice* as old."

And in an odd way, that math made more sense than he knew, since we probably passed each other in some sort of orbit of age years ago, about the time my mother died. Before, he was the obvious authority—someone I turned to for guidance on tax shelters and car maintenance. When Gwen and I were just starting to hunt for houses, we both called our fathers for some advice. Later, when I asked what she learned, she shook her head and grimaced. "He said something about 'escrow' and lost me." I smiled back. "My dad talked about 'equity.'"

After that, though, after I saw my father cry at my mother's service, our roles somewhat reversed. That was the first day I just felt old—old in that familial, social, cultural way. It had little to do with physical age. Traveling through that horrendous event seemed to have warped space and time, such that my father and I reversed directions: he becoming increasingly younger, more boyish and carefree, more lost in the past; me trending toward safety, watchfulness, more careful of the ground underneath my feet, yes, but also underneath his.

To me the crane games were some of the most pleasant episodes I had with my father, and it was not sheer diversion, mere escape from inevitable discussions of economic woes, the future of coal or of the planet in general. There was probably a willful sort of return for me, too, not to my own childhood exactly but rather all the way back to his. The gleam in his eye, the care with which he tended to the contraption's constant breakdowns (broken rubber bands, derailed pulleys).

Care, sensitivity, *tending to:* these are scientific, logical, rational iterations of love.

Jupiter has no fixed, solid core, at least not to our knowledge. Under its clouds, the planet harbors a 13,000-mile-deep layer of hydrogen and helium, which, gradually—under extreme pressure—turns those gasses to liquids. Below that, another liquid layer—this time 25,000 miles deep—of metallic hydrogen. Beneath that, who knows? a rocky core, maybe?

Some theorize that if such a solid center did exist, it would be larger than Earth and thirty times its mass, the pressure and heat amazing. The numbers do not make sense: 55,000 degrees Fahrenheit. Jupiter is nearly the twin of our Sun, in fact. (It's that big.) Plus a galaxy with just one star is a rarity. Jupiter should have fired up. We should have *two* burning orbs in our skies.

Gin yer hert be cauld, read my grandfather's fireplace mantel, *a canna warm ye.* How did we grow apart, father and son? Or did we just stubbornly hold to our old patterns, unable to show affection the way my mother and I did so effortlessly? My father and I were close in the way workmates are, those who share a space and a common endeavor for years but rarely socialize outside the office. We were close the way two planets are close, warming themselves by similar light, tracing different orbits that, only at choice instances—once, twice a year—bring them close enough to see each other clearly.

My sister and cousin took most of the Snow Village models. My cousin still displays them all—my mother's collection mixed with her own, including the little toy shop that once sat on our table, where I would have peered into its false windows and imagined some fabulous, wind-up bounty, skaters cutting their endless figures on a mirror outside.

I walk around our neighborhood here in Georgia—most of the houses midcentury—and easily pick out the tear-downs, the rebuilds, the places *not of* this place. With the kitschy Snow Village houses, though, the timelessness is unnerving, much like the odd sense of familiarity that washed over me in that room in the Scottish inn. Familiar, that is, until I opened the curtains and saw where I really was.

That entire Scotland trip was a study in paradoxes: the blank, onyx face of that night near Fort William giving way to a treeless, alien landscape the next day; the forbidding moodiness and bulbous mountains glowering over us in our curiously bright-green rental van, as we threaded through the glens; the dark, rich beer salving the bite of an Islay single malt. Layers upon layers of foreignness.

Small wonder, then, when we reached Helensburgh, birthplace of my father's father, and his father before that—names receding into the distance like burning comets—that it, too, made us feel not of that place, rendered us alien. The cemetery did at least, which took us a few pub owners and gas station attendants to find. (This was before GPS and the ubiquity of navigational aids, global tracking systems, and hordes of satellites.) Rows and rows of headstones—massive, slabby, and lichen-riddled—lay toppled in the spongy ground, some slowly working back into the earth, shape-shifting.

Vandals, a caretaker told us. Boys drunk and bored with anger. Boys against history, against their own inevitable smallness and, finally, obliteration. Alien, too, the way we somehow found our name, my great-grandfather's marker, the letters scarcely legible, there among those toppled stones. I remember that my mother—having learned a little trick from her sister's genealogical field work—went back to the van to retrieve a can of shaving cream and then spread it across the face of the stone, pushing it into the grooves of letters. When we scraped away the excess, the name THOMAS DAVIDSON became perfectly visible.

No way that rock was coming up, though. My father, Ben, and I huddled around its top, our fingers crimped underneath. Together we could raise it maybe six inches, but gravity just pulled it back. Gwen, my mother, and aunt—all strangely buoyant—giggled at our labor, offered mock encouragement. And yet, involved in our hopeless task, we finally felt part of that Northern land, part of its ground and atmosphere. The afternoon was oddly humid, I remember, the air not warm exactly but rather thick. We panted and laughed. We peeled off our sweaters, draped them over my mother's arms, and tried in earnest, knees in the muck, brows muddied, all three of us past that critical point when staining clothes or breaking a sweat mattered anymore. We had committed ourselves to the endeavor. Still nothing. The stone's density and mass overwhelmed us.

"Wait," Ben said, "what about a car jack?" Could we even prop the slab enough to slide the thing underneath? And wouldn't the jack itself sink into the soft ground, just as these heavy stones were busy doing? Besides, how high would an extended car jack get us? Part of me, even then, imagined a trip to the emergency room in Glasgow: crushed fingers, broken bones. My father, though, seemed to be mulling it over, busy contemplating the fix.

"You may have an idea, there," he said, and motioned for us to retrieve the jack.

When we returned, he had found a few half-rotten boards. "Gives us some mechanical advantage," he said, holding them up.

Maybe the jack in that cartoonishly green van was simply bulkier, beefier, with a longer range. Maybe the salvaged boards offered that final inch or two of leverage. Maybe. In any case, after my father carefully positioned the jack on a board and slid it under the struggle of Ben and me holding the stone off the ground; after we nervously extended the central post, click after click after click, to its maximum height; only then could the three of us heave and cross that barrier of gravity, careful not to let the momentum carry the stone past plumb, let it crash down on its face. There's a photo of us around the marker, all of us—Ben, my parents, my aunt, Gwen, and I. And my great-grandfather, I suppose, too.

And the vast distances my father and I had traveled to return to the site of our making.

The Juno probe is scheduled to finish its mission in September 2025, by which time it will have orbited the oldest and largest planet circling our Sun well over the originally planned thirty-two times, dutifully sending back data after each pass, adding to our understanding not only of the gas giant itself but of the formation of our solar system.

Radiation levels, however, in Jupiter's magnetosphere—through which Juno passes as it nears the planet—are quite high and will, over time, inevitably cause partial and full instrument failures. Once that occurs, the risk of collision with one of Jupiter's moons increases. NASA has thus planned for Juno's ultimate task to be a controlled deorbit into the Jovian atmosphere. It's a suicide mission of sorts, at least for the craft itself, which will burn up, disintegrate in atmospheric friction, becoming unrecognizable soot and carbon dust, maybe a few diamonds, all of it part of Jupiter itself, or whatever lies under all that cloud.

No Business

We had no business kayaking. We were short on time and gear. Robert's rental truck lacked straps, even eyeholes in the bed to help secure the boats, which we also had to rent. The woman at the sporting-goods store grimaced when we said as much, reluctantly loaning us some rope and frayed tie-downs. Mid-twenties, tan and fit, almost taut, she wore her baseball hat backward, keeping her stringy brown hair off her face as she helped me load the kayaks in the truck.

"You going all the way to Kintla?" she asked, barely able to conceal her disapproval, squinting in the late-morning glare. "Good luck with that."

We had no business driving over two hours each way, mostly on unpaved logging roads, to a remote launch on Kintla Lake, one of the more secluded in Glacier National Park. A promise, however, is a promise, and Robert—who hosted us at his house in Whitefish—had promised Gwen and me the experience, along with myriad others that week (scenic hikes, mountain biking with his son-in-law, meals at all his favorite places).

"It's a bit far to go, sure," he said in the truck as we left the store, "but wait until you see it."

He had scheduled our last few days in Montana almost to the hour, cramming everything he wanted us to see and do. We would have at best a few hours on the lake. Not really worth the trouble, but what the hell, we thought.

"Wait until you see Kintla," he repeated, smiling, as we left the paved road ten miles past the park's west entrance, kicking up dust, bleached and fine as flour.

A man steals a plane, steals it from a busy, international airport. An airline employee—a guy who handles bags, de-ices wings—just climbs into the cockpit and, whoosh, takes off. The plane, a Q400 Turboprop, can hold seventy-six passengers but is believed empty, reports say, when the man ascends over Puget Sound from Sea-Tac. "Believed empty," they say, and belief is, in this case, inconsequential, vacuous. The facts are too heavy, substantive; they weigh; they possess gravity. For instance: that this ground-crew member has not in any way trained as a pilot. Says he learned what little he knows from playing video games, flying simulators. Says this to officials over the radio as he flies.

Says a lot, actually. Keeps talking, chatty, in what one official later refers to as "a frenzied stream of consciousness." He talks about how beautiful the Olympic Mountains look, if he might go to jail, and why he's burned through fuel so quickly. Says he'd hoped for "a moment of serenity" in the Turboprop, in the sky.

This all occurs minutes before the plane crashes on Ketron Island, southwest of the airport. Photos show a wooded area on fire, the debris field.

"A joy ride," some local official says, "gone terribly wrong." Surely a perverse use of the word *joy*.

And yet videos, recorded by onlookers, show the plane diving, looping, and rolling over Puget Sound at sunset.

The road from Apgar to Kintla, flanking Glacier's western boundary, follows the North Fork of the Flathead River, glimpses of which we caught to our right. Mostly, though, we worried about the rented kayaks, which hopped around, slipping in the truck bed. We worried, too, about what seemed an inordinate number of cyclists, especially for a fairly well-trafficked dirt road. Bandannas pulled over their mouths, they appeared out of the very dust clouds themselves, as if conjured from the air, their saddlebags overloaded with gear, everything coated in gray, ashen powder.

"That looks horrible," Gwen said, and I had to agree. While big trucks whizzed past, the cyclists rode through a complete whiteout. Even safely, comfortably in our cab, we still had to keep distance between us and the next truck for fear of losing sight of the road itself.

"Can't they find a better place to bike?" Gwen asked.

Robert and I shrugged. She sat back in her seat, clearly annoyed.

People often do things just to do them, just because. No reason. That's at least the reason I offered her.

She shook her head. "I'd rather drive a school bus."

When a plane full of people goes down, we call the passengers *souls,* as in "276 souls aboard," bodies themselves simply forms of transport, mere vehicles, not parts of a debris field on a windswept plain in Scotland, strewn in plastic and metal on a Russian steppe, in a shorn cornfield in Iowa, on a scorched bit of island near Seattle, pines like stubble, charred and fidgety in the gusts.

Normal operations at Sea-Tac resume quickly. Planes have stacked up—forty all told—awaiting clearance. Passengers probably annoyed. Things to do. No time for a joy ride. Two F-15 fighter pilots—dispatched, poised, ready to shoot the Turboprop down if the pilot (a kid, really, a baggage handler), if he threatened to use the plane like a missile—return to their base. I imagine those trained pilots, probably not much older than the joy rider, retelling the story, almost inexplicable, that evening. Stories, at least the kind we retell, tend to be inexplicable, which is why we keep retelling them, turning them over in our minds, appraising their features, looking for slight tears, weaknesses, ways in, or through, or out of.

Sometimes we have to dismantle a thing to really understand it.

Halfway to Kintla, Robert took a right and asked if we were hungry. We had not seen anything along that road but big trucks and SUVs, a few private cabins, some masochistic cyclists. Where were we going to eat up there, an hour down a dirt road to nowhere?

"You'll see," he said. "Place has been around forever."

Polebridge Mercantile, unless you have witnessed it; unless you fantasize about living off the grid with live bluegrass and exquisitely baked muffins and bear claws; unless your dream of a hippie commune involves camping in a dusty lot or renting one of the tiny cabins surrounding the store, in an open flood-plain off the North Fork, in the far northwest corner of Glacier and of the state of Montana itself, not ten miles from the Canadian border; unless any of that, the place is difficult to describe. With its Old West–style storefront, its stoop and slanted wooden awning—POLEBRIDGE MERCANTILE in large white letters relieved from an ox-blood clapboard façade—the building seemed plopped down in that treeless, featureless expanse; a Main Street general store without any Main Street, not even a paved thoroughfare. The business had no business being there.

Big trucks, however, piled in the parking lots to either side of its entrance, as hordes of cyclists choked up the road to lean their bikes on the side of the building, swatting dust from their neon gear before joining us inside. Simply being there, amid the comforts of freshly baked everything, seemed transgressive, flukish, rare. How could a place like this exist?

"You kidding me?" Robert said. "They're open year round."

He gestured to framed photos on the walls, attesting to that fact: the building, its slew of cabins and a not unimpressive music stage, the entire ghastly plain robed in four feet of snow, business booming.

We chewed on muffins and sticky buns as we left Polebridge, heading farther north. I felt vaguely sick to my stomach. Perhaps the muffin. Perhaps the almost invisible effects of a wildfire still burning in Canada, in Idaho. Somewhere, it seemed, something was always burning, producing that faintly sweet, nauseating smell of cinder, of danger and destruction.

But maybe, too, my unease was simpler: just that unsettling sense of dread, of my father somewhere at the moment fretting the cancer, wondering where it was traveling, where it had no business being. Just as we probably had no business being where we were. Trespassing, it almost felt like, bringing our overly cheery kayaks (boats of leisure, surely) and our big truck along the North Fork and continuing to Kintla Lake, driving right into the heart of nowhere specific.

How easily, really, we trespass, ending up where we have no business. How little stands in our way. All the complexities of a modern airplane, not to mention concentric rings of airport security. Even then, a ground employee simply walks on, starts the engines, taxis, and takes off.

When my mother wanted to imply bravado in a transgression, she used the verb *waltz*, as in, "They say the guy just *waltzed* right in and stole the money." And I suppose the joy ride approximates that: a bit of art, a dance, his looping and rolling over Puget Sound, one show only, live and uncut.

"I got a lot of people that care about me," the baggage handler admits over the radio. "It's gonna disappoint them to hear that I did this."

All that, and still the worry over others, that he had crossed some invisible, final border, had misbehaved in the eyes of those who cared for him.

"Just a broken guy," he says, "a few screws loose."

Part of me thought we would never kayak, that we would arrive at the remote boat launch and not find parking. Crazy, I know, way up there, but the campground bordering the lake was indeed full.

"Never seen it this way," the on-duty ranger told us, leaning his left arm on Robert's rearview mirror. Nowhere to park, he said, but maybe we could tuck behind those trash bins by the restroom.

"I won't rat on you," he added playfully, kicking a few rocks from the asphalt lot.

I unstrapped the boats while Robert and Gwen—shocked a bit by our near failure—gathered supplies from the cab. Hours to prepare—a rather easy, inconsequential kayak jaunt—and still we discussed if we needed food, where the sunscreen was, who had an extra hat, the sun blinding us. We all acted dazed, exposed suddenly to the outside air, to a pristine, glacial lake and the incongruous sound of kids splashing in the cordoned-off shallows.

Beautiful, for sure, that clear water, the shore pine-lined and boulder-flanked. And yet the sky, opaque, felt heavy as a blanket. I remembered the last time my father and I were in the mountains together, sitting on the porch of a rental cabin outside Purgatory, Colorado, listening to the shrieks of the red-taileds. I remembered, too, that sickly sweet smell of wildfires from my childhood in California, the worry in my parents' voices, the flashes of red on the brown hillside above our house and my father soaking our cedar-shake roof, tiny embers floating in the very air we breathed.

"Must be the fires," Robert said, shaking his head, clearly disappointed.

Above the lake, where one usually admired the mountains of northwest Glacier—Long Knife, Kinnerly, Kintla Peak, ridged and, even in August, snow-capped—we saw only a weighty, beige, ineffable, formless sadness.

"I'm so sorry," Robert added, and we felt worse for his feeling that way, all three of us a little out of sorts, as we pushed off from the shore.

The White House press secretary commended what she called "the interagency response effort, the protection of public safety." Governor Jay Inslee of Washington applauded the Air National Guard from Washington and Oregon for dispatching the jets. People thanked other people in a chain of gratitude that welled out from the event, rippling as if from the center of a lake. Pleasing when things come to an end, when we can wash our hands of it all. "Finding closure," we often say, though the fact that a man walked on a commercial plane—*waltzed* on—and just took off: that opens up rifts, creates holes. Difficult to wrap it all up, make sense.

I keep seeing his deep dive over the water: the elegance, the poetry when he pulls up just in time, almost skimming across the water, then ascending steeply again. Suicidal but poetic.

We fool ourselves when we think of those two states as oppositional: suicidal, poetic. They are interrelated, smoke and fire, body and soul.

Imagine a wide, featureless, desert, perhaps some low-slung gray-brown mountains in the distance, a cluster of shrubs, the eerie if caricature-like humanness of Saguaros studding the nothingness. Imagine the nearly endless stretch of sand now dotted—no, absolutely replete—with golf balls, tens of thousands of them, maybe more, cast across that desperately forbidding sameness.

Vince once asked me to imagine that, said he saw it himself driving trains from Tucson to Yuma, as he did throughout his twenties and thirties. A train hauling golf balls had partially derailed somewhere outside Sentinel, Arizona, creating a kind of art installation, a transgression of the everyday.

I wrote to him recently to make sure I remembered it correctly, that I remembered *his remembering it* correctly, that he had actually witnessed the golf balls in the desert. Yes, he said, exactly right. That and a load of Sega Genesis video-game consoles still in their boxes, in what must have appeared the aftermath of a boat gone down, the flotsam of a tragedy just before Christmas, in the Sonoran Desert.

"Lots of rail-track workers' kids got a special present under the tree that year," he wrote. "It was funny," he added, in that way we refer to the odd occurrence: not comical but unexpected, uncanny. Still makes us smile, even if we don't understand why.

I keep seeing those golf balls, though, their surfaces pocked like tiny moons, the absolute stillness of them, some sort of mystical desert bloom. Part of me might call the scene beautiful but of a difficult variety. All that leisure and privilege wrapped inside a rubber-cored ball—ubiquitous as money and signifying similarly—lost, tossed out, spurned, jettisoned, exiled in the desert. The golf balls had no business being there, which is precisely the allure.

"And you who are living yet," Charon commands Dante at the shores of Acheron, "begone from these who are dead." This scene happens early in *The Inferno*, but the trope recurs often, this calling out of Dante by a denizen of hell, that Dante should not be there.

"By other windings and by other steerage," Charon continues, "shall you cross to that other shore. Not here! Not here!"

A professor of mine once gestured in class at these moments in Dante's narrative. The entire epic, he said, is one of transgression.

Dante had no business being there.

We marveled at Kintla's crystalline water. How deep was that desiccated tree trunk underneath us? Ten feet? Could have been fifty, really, with nothing at all to obscure our view of the lake's nearly lunar bottom.

I took the lead, hugged the coastline, following what I thought was a cedar waxwing but which could have also been a robin. (I couldn't get close enough to tell.) It flitted among pine branches stretched over the shore, toying with me, or so it seemed.

After a while, I drifted into the middle of that scythe-shaped and deeply gouged lake. Gwen and Robert followed at a distance, none of us in a hurry to be anywhere, by then enjoying the gentle sway of our kayaks, the dull light from a cloud-absorbed and smoke-choked sun casting an almost aluminum-like sheen across the water.

I concentrated on some fallen debris on the far shore, wondered about the current, tried to discern if I was moving away from or toward those shallows. I repositioned the nose of the boat, pointing it directly at the toppled pine, perhaps a birch or two pulled down with the larger tree, all of them bent over and half-sunk, a disruption in that otherwise pristine coastline. Gwen and Robert had moved on, or they were right behind me. I couldn't tell.

What happened next I find difficult to explain. No sudden wind kicked up and threatened my boat. No freak storm or lightning strike. No grizzly. Not even a hawk's fitful cry or the leap of some exuberant fish. The boat launch, safe in the distance, gave no sound, no kids splashing about on blow-up toys. Not a leaf stir, wave lap, my own kayak undulating, bird call or plane engine.

None of that but rather the sudden absence, the vacuum, the totalizing force of silence. I floated in a scene with the sound turned off.

Maybe I am making more of it than I should. Big deal if suddenly the breeze, the movement of the water, the leaves in the trees, if suddenly all of that vanished, a washed-out sky descending on the lake like a hush. And yet Robert felt it too.

"Wasn't that *odd?*" he asked as we paddled back to the launch. "I sat there and heard *nothing,*" he said, "not even my own breath."

Not unpleasant exactly, that strange feeling of otherness, of some small trespass into midday, on a lake saturated in blunt light and caught in a trance. Not unpleasant, but.

Later at dinner, Robert's wife asked if we had enjoyed the trip. I watched Robert consider that word *enjoy,* almost repeating it to himself. He felt the need to clarify, too, to calibrate the question in some way that could more accurately probe our kayaking on Kintla. He smiled at me and then looked at her, tilting his head to one side.

"It was," he paused, "interesting," then tapped his knife lightly on the thick plastic cup of water in front of him.

The restaurant resembled an old hunting lodge. We ate retro food: martinis and wedge salads, steaks and river fish. And though we all tried to recount the entire experience, it still remained outside the comfortable outlines of a story.

Kayaking on Lake Kintla, the afternoon itself, behaved more like a transgression.

☠

"Though no man can draw a stroke between the confines of day and night," Edmund Burke wrote, "yet light and darkness are upon the whole tolerably distinguishable."

Difficult to tell the exact moment when everything changes. Something changed in me that afternoon, that moment, that knife's edge between who I was before the silence and who kayaked off the lake. Now—in the absence my father's death has created for me—I cannot tell if I am the person who experienced that odd kayaking trip or the person writing about it. Not that I look back on Lake Kintla as some defining moment. And I don't trust such radical moments of mutation much anymore. Small trespasses, rather, tiny transgressions seem more palpable, less easily defined, less given to mythologies. We almost half-create them, manufacture the tiny tears in the fabric our lives are cloaked in, out of the stream of the happening. We might even seek that exile, fearing the constant movement of the everyday, its current strong, unlike the calm waters of Kintla.

Because I read about the man stealing the plane, I read about him that very night, after dinner, while we sat on Robert's porch. Because the kid climbed aboard that plane not long after our Kintla trip. Because despite the constant warnings to him not to trespass, Dante does it anyway, makes it through hell, its deepest reaches frozen, the bodies of sinners caught in ice, inert, like insects in amber. All that stasis; that rigid, ancient, horrifying beauty.

Because by morning, airplanes traced anew their contrails in the sky above Sea-Tac, business as usual. Because legend claims that a man drowned in Kintla Lake, entered its waters and never returned, that the waters closed over him. Which is why the word *kintla*—of Kutenai origin—means *sack.*

Because sacks are good for holding things together, holding onto them, holding them in, or holding them under.

Unsent Letter to the Living #2

Dear XXXXX,

Thank you for the words you shared at my father's service last week. My younger brother surely appreciated them, as he stood with his head bowed, shifting his weight from side to side. My older sister, who sat on my lap—not enough chairs for all the people, turns out—must have also loved your words, your narrative of my father's sudden spiritual awakening, since she kept kicking the insides of my ankles, squeezing my leg, as if to signal how deeply your story resonated, her own body a vessel not large enough to contain the joy in your recalling my father's final day, and how he, in your words, accepted Christ into his heart, there at the quivering lip of eternity.

The whole day seemed suddenly expansive. Circle after circle of friends and family gathered, interlocked, eating together in my father's house, which used to be my parents' house, which is where we had all gathered—my father included—eight years earlier, after my mother's death, our first day in that strange, new kingdom.

I'm sure you knew this when you—someone I had never met, the wife of one of my father's coworkers—when you asked to speak to everyone, family and fast neighbors, folks we knew well. You told your story of redemption, of my father—a lifelong atheist—somehow, at your bidding, miraculously accepting Christ into his heart. Thank the Lord you were there to facilitate. We must thank the Lord for everything, is what you said. I think you said *the Lord* sixteen times, but my sister was kicking me, and I cannot be sure.

What I can be sure of, based on your testimony, is that my father—a lifelong, silent, scientific atheist—accepted Christ into his heart and—*voilà!*—instant salvation, puffy clouds and all.

It suddenly seems urgent that I explain to you the etymology of *voilà*, a French term that marries the imperative form of the verb *voir* (*to see*) with *là*, which means *there* and is technically an adverb, though I know that sounds odd. Because, you see, more than a cliché for something (was it a rabbit?) conjured out of the hat of a magician—some mustachioed chap in a black cloak, a bloke who resembles not at all Jesus Christ—*voilà* also captures your odd story, your oddly *familiar* story of someone (in this case my father) whose forsaken soul was suddenly saken—*voilà!*—under Christ's all-seeing gaze, there in a nondescript if comfortable room, on the fourth floor of the Baylor Medical Center, in Grapevine, Texas.

Thank you for your impassioned witnessing of my father's salvation, on the last day of his life; for your explanation using the language of the Bible, a book about which my father knew little, his truths coming instead through ohms and wattage, the pleasure of a well-soldered circuit, the hum of a big-block engine, or the elegance of a lightbulb filled not with oxygen but with argon, a gas that prevents corrosion of its tungsten filament, which burns an eerie purple-blue. The precision of it all. The engineering.

The way my father looked upon a radio he rebuilt, the smoldering glow of its tubes: that's the closest he came to any rapture he'd allow himself. I can't tell you how many times I saw him look at a transistor or a torque wrench that way, but I can tell you that Abraham looked up and there in a thicket saw a ram caught by its horns. He later slaughtered that ram.

Yes, we, his children, had departed for our homes in three different states by the time you arrived at the hospital that day. We were gone, "scattered among all peoples," says the Bible, "serving other gods, wood and stone." We knew that the end, no matter the specific time, was inevitable, and that our being there, as opposed to anywhere, meant very little. We were simply taking up space, matter itself, while our father was, in some sense, already gone, departed dearly, almost immaterial, technically alive but just, the hospital having ceased treatment while increasing dosages of drugs I'd never heard of, drugs whose names sounded antique and slightly mythic, like the names for noble gases, or tributaries to rivers in the underworld, or lame gods in search of vengeance in labyrinths made of the bones of the undeserving. But I digress.

I digress as my father did that final day, jacked up on pain meds, his insides metastatic and roiling, the far shore in view, the end approaching. As Pharaoh approached, says the Bible, the Israelites looked up, and—*voilà!*—there were the Egyptians, marching after them. I added the *voilà,* but the Israelites were certainly terrified and cried out to the Lord something akin. Not sure it did much good.

Just as I am not sure that the smoothie I made—cacao nibs, banana, oatmeal, nut milk, and chia; a sort of jacked-up chocolate milk my father loved—not sure the smoothie was anywhere near perfect or idealized, hardly manna from heaven, though that's what my father called it, "just perfect," he said—his final words to me, turns out—eyes closed, relishing its chalk and grit, its sweet, cold creaminess, as he sipped it a few hours before we left, before you arrived with your preconstructed, antique narrative, which is the way the Lord Himself arrived to the Israelites. While fleeing their persecutors in the sands (as I am sure you know), Aaron spoke to the whole exiled community, who looked toward the desert, and there—*voilà!*—was the glory of the Lord, burning a cool purple-blue.

You said that you spoke to my father and asked him to accept Christ into his heart, which I am sure he did, which is to say that I am sure whatever confirmation you wanted to see (and hear) you saw (and heard)—*voilà!*—there on the fourth floor of the Oncology Tower, in that quiet, nondescript room. Though to be fair, just that morning my father had moaned as we, his children, spoke of our travel plans and fretted leaving him, unsure of anything but the surety of his impending death—maybe hours, maybe days, maybe weeks, no one knew—my brother shifting from leg to leg, my sister squeezing the air out of the room with her constant petting of him.

He moaned, and when we asked repeatedly what was wrong, if he was in pain, he simply said, after a long pause, that, no, no pain, but that, sometimes, he just felt like moaning, enunciating, letting us know, for as long as he could—*voilà!, look!*—that he was not gone, not yet, was still there, while each subsequent nurse arrived, replacing the previous nurse's name with her own on the white board by the door.

You said in front of all our family and friends that you asked my father—a lifelong, silent, scientific, unobtrusive, don't-make-a-fuss-about-me, believe-whatever-you-want-but-keep-me-out-of-it athe-ist—that you asked him to accept Christ into his heart, though surely he and his heart were too busy accepting jacked-up amounts of drugs that mask pain while slowing the heart, lowering its pressure, lulling it to sleep.

How much accepting, finally, can any heart do? That's what my sister's kicks and squeezings, my brother's looking down at his shoes as if kicking an imaginary rabbit skull back and forth, that's what they seemed to ask, while you carried on coolly with your salvation narrative, like the Israelites did the burden of their belief.

You said that you asked my father to accept Christ into his heart that day—his last day—after my brother, my sister, and I had departed. (You were specific about that chronology, repeated it for what seemed dramatic effect—we, the deserters, the unbelievers.) Meanwhile we were in cars and planes, in transit, in exile from the kingdom we all came from, or surely we would have borne witness to your fantastical correction to the eternal ledger, made in the blocky caps of an engineer, the box checked next to the word SAVED.

And he was, I believe, saved, saved at least from understanding any of what you said, your words by then whirling in the air around his bed like the anonymous souls of the damned in Dante's *Inferno*, a book about which my father also knew little though just enough to under-stand that it's fiction, spiritual hocus pocus; that Dante just engineered his own salvation, gamed the system, pulled himself out of a deep, black hole. *Voila!*

I *do* know that book, though, and most of the diabolical punishments—the ones that really keep me up at night—have to do with language and the misuses of it; the terror and humiliation such acts engender; the petty, sanctimonious, self-serving, boorish, corrosive grandstanding that still goes on, eternally, even if we all, Dante included, die and are burned, or are drained of our fluids and buried in the dirt.

Dante's bones? Now that truly *was* a mystery. Some lucky fool discovered them centuries later, in Ravenna. The folks there are still not budging. Each year they twist the daggers of their praise just a little further into the heart of Florence, where Dante was born and from which he was exiled. I have visited his grave, as well as the hell he imagined. I think you would like it.

By the way, I also have that argon bulb—one of my father's favorites—and it burns with a singular, purple-blue, scientifically explainable grace.

Sincerely,
Chad

Golden Boy

It could have been muffler repair. It could have been porn or guns. Instead it's a coffeehouse, which my brother, who lives close by, frequents on his way to work. Brings his own fancy-pants mug with him. Drinks coffee with the other regulars. Golden Boy, the place is called, where they serve up all the latest pour-overs and cold brews; cortados from monocultures picked, roasted, and sent in burlap, I supposed, to that dingy-faced concrete-floored whatever-you-want-to-call-it—coffeehouse, café, bar (they serve cocktails in the evenings, grilled cheese at lunch)—with velvet paintings on the walls, stacks of board games on butcher racks, and Bob Ross on the flat screen's perpetual loop, playing God with the ghostly white of his canvases. Pine and alder and spruce and a desperate kind of lakefront isolation.

My brother, sister, and I sipped our overpriced coffees, picked over scones. It was how we mourned our father that day, what mourning looked like not two months after his death. There in Texas to sift through the house and our own shared past, we procrastinated and dallied, huddled in that warm place, with warm drinks, warm television, while outside the temperatures dropped and the pissing rain pissed sideways, covered everything in drear.

My brother gabbed with some scraggly-haired guy, a beat-up laptop open and glowing in front of him. Stickers from what I gathered were local bands plastered the machine's backside. The two of them talked honey and beekeeping. One of the other regulars, whom they both knew well (everyone knows everyone else there), was a beekeeper. Strangely, out of sheer happenstance, honeycombs adorned the place, and cocktails featured honey prominently. My brother, in fact, was wearing a hat from the beekeeper friend.

Stylized honeycombs. Gold on gold.

My sister and I stared at the baristas. They buzzed around.

"I get tired," she said, "just looking at them."

And I was tired of missing our father, of pretending everything was fine. Sure, we got together, the three of us, and instantly fell into our old routines, our familiar registers, talking over one another, inhabiting old jokes and stories. But that was simply a way to survive now: keeping busy. Worker bees.

Over forty years together, the three of us, means it's hard to break habits. And a place devoted to serving a low-level, socially acceptable drug was, I suppose, fitting for such talk of ritual, of crutch, of predilections both good and bad. I was spinning from the sugary scone, the juiced-up coffee.

The two kids behind the bar—I can't remember their names, though I remember my brother recounting their backstories later in the car—they got chatty, joshed with my brother about how much he and I look alike (which we do, sort of), while my sister smiled. She busied herself trying to snap a photo of the three of us, her arm outstretched. She could not quite fit us all in, what with the memory of our father intruding, taking up space. The frame was too crowded.

Bob Ross was finishing a squat cabin at the head of a cove, its reflection shimmering. He was pleased with his efforts, I could tell. He was so damn happy he glowed.

"Here," my sister finally said to me, handing over her phone, "your arm's longer."

In that photo, she is on the left, with a serene, velvet tiger peering out from the subway-tiled wall behind her. My brother, sandwiched between us, seems a kind of painting himself, almost part of the backdrop, curiously similar in expression to a velvet lion—regal, indifferent—which hung to his side. And then there's me, smiling awkwardly from the right, my arm reaching out to point the camera back at us.

Unshaven and beanie-adorned, I'm dressed in the most fabulously ludicrous, metallic-yellow jacket.

"Hey, look," my brother said to me right after I snapped the photo, gesturing toward my new winter wear: "You're wearing a golden boy in Golden Boy."

●

And I was.

I was wearing a golden (more mustard-yellow), space-age, lightweight, fancy-pants hoodie my sister brought me from Portland. It was like wearing muted sunlight. Diffused, early-winter sunlight slanting through spindles of trees. It was like wearing a color only notionally of this world. Bob Ross would have probably mixed Yellow Ochre with just a daub of Indian Yellow. I swear, in certain light, even a horse-hair's breadth of Phthalo Green. Hints of Midnight Black.

A difficult color. A synthesized color, hard and labored over.

Seems all the rage. At least that's what my sister had said when we talked two months before. Something about a friend giving her a special pass to the Columbia employee store, how it felt vaguely criminal, just being there.

"Stuff is so cheap," she said. I could hear the little whizzing gizmos of commerce behind her: intercom fuss, the slide of hangers over metal racks, chatter of the electronic check-out. "I can't believe how cheap it is."

There was, in fact, much about the time around our father's death that seemed unbelievable: for instance how we all still had lives—my sister, my brother, and I—and spouses, and houses, and jobs. Routines. How winter had indeed returned again, after a prolonged autumn. How it all just seemed to carry on, repeating endlessly, like the Bob Ross loop. Those episodes in Golden Boy, though: they calmed me, calmed everyone, even with the audio muted in deference to the barista's retro, lo-fi playlist (Pavement, Guided by Voices, Sebadoh) and the constant rumble of the milk frother. All strangely familiar yet also unbelievable.

Unbelievable: that's what Ross himself might have said, too, about his curious afterlife in hipster bars and coffee joints. Born in 1942, to a Cherokee carpenter and a waitress, in Daytona Beach, Florida, he would not, in fact, have immediately struck anyone as a calming influence, let alone a precocious, artistic talent. Never the kind of celebrity around which an industry might later be erected. Golden boys don't drop out of school in the ninth grade. Golden boys don't work with fathers on construction jobs, lose parts of their fingers in accidents. (Pay attention in those videos; note the peculiar way in which Ross holds the palette in his left—and partially mutilated—hand.)

If that were a less than auspicious start for the artist, Ross—aged eighteen—then joined the Air Force, where he served for twenty years, eventually reaching the rank of Master Sergeant. He became the cliché we all know: the fastidious, meticulously-creased-pants-wearing heckler of recruits; toppler of messy bunks; the guy demanding that those clean-shaven pansies drop and give him twenty. He despised the permed hair that became his trademark, preferring always the crew-cut military style he had grown up wearing. (The perm, through happenstance, became part of his iconic look and, thus, indispensable to the industry.)

And maybe it was that sense of retro before retro was cool, kitsch before kitsch itself became an economy, a way of being. Maybe it was Bob Ross's timelessness, as if he had walked out of some transcendental hippie mountain village in the foothills of '60s California, and right into American living rooms. Maybe his subtle complexity, nearly invisible in those videos; the sense that, beyond that soft, nurturing exterior, existed some capacious, contemplative intelligence. Maybe that's why we needed him, why he had returned.

My father, years ago, would sometimes sit and watch Bob Ross episodes with my brother and me. We mouthed Ross's best lines together ("happy little trees," etc.), smirked whenever he banged his wet brush on the

vultures all having fed, the house by then—at least what remained—just a few trips to the landfill shy of complete and utter emptiness, cold and wintry itself.

As was that painting my brother had attempted. No house, no cabin, no sign of habitation: a terrifying scene, really, bereft of the human. No wonder none of us could bear to possess it. No wonder we could not throw it away. It was a terrible painting, to which my brother would also attest, but terrible in that word's full semantic register, its broader, more expansive significance, the same terror we felt entering my father's house after he died and the walls almost constricted, as the world outside chilled and grew darker.

A few months prior to my father's death, the machinery of winter seemed utterly incoherent, thrown out of whack. Bizarre days at our home near Atlanta: seventy, eighty degrees; freak rains and thunder late at night; short sleeves and sweat on the neck.

And not just weather and temperature but also rituals, traditions disrupted. My father's health made Thanksgiving together at our place—a tradition we had started after my mother died—difficult. He hadn't been well enough to fly or drive the entire year, really. But since Gwen and I have no children and my siblings celebrate mostly with their own families, I figured we could just come to him in Texas. It would be earlier in the month, because of work and commitments, but who cared?

"Sounds great," he had said. We would bring Thanksgiving—albeit in anticipation—to him. "Great," he repeated. "Would love to have you."

When his condition deteriorated, when my brother, sister, and I started to parcel out time with him, ensure that someone always kept vigil, I booked another weekend, a few weeks before the Thanksgiving trip. Sitting in his den, I remember gently chiding him about the disorder.

"You have to keep the house up, dad," I said, gesturing at the newspapers piled on the kitchen table, the bundles of soiled bedding in the laundry room, the harshly antiseptic smell.

"I know, I know," he said, rubbing his feet together nervously, head nodding side to side in his recliner, eyes closed. He kept his hands face down on the armrests, as if bracing for something.

All I could do was clean, keep positive, ignore what I knew was serious. He had been in and out of the hospital. He required nearly constant tending, even at home. "I'm so glad you're here," he said.

At night, after he dozed off, I devised jogging routes for myself and strategized pace, the minutiae of my arbitrary running schedule. Mornings, before he woke, I laced up and took to the road, diligently ticking off the day's mileage, working off anxiety. Even then, late October, the hard, penetrating, Texas sunlight. Afterward, panting and sweating in small puddles, I chugged Gatorade on his back deck.

Strange heat: stagnant, heavy, sluggish. Enough to make me fear for the planet itself, which was probably just displaced fear for my father, who rose later in the day, had little appetite, and tired far too easily. The entire situation, outside temperature included, seemed to be heating up, not cooling down. Such that when my sister called to say that she would be visiting the Columbia employee store, that lots of great brands—fancy-pants brands like Prana and Mountain Hardwear—were stupid cheap, and that if I needed or wanted anything to let her know, the thought of asking for a new winter jacket seemed preposterous.

Be forward thinking, I thought to myself later, as I cooked chili to freeze for my father, threw out expired pantry items without his spotting me. *Just because it's warm now,* I reasoned, *won't be for long.* My current winter jacket sucked. I hated it. I coveted a coworker's oddly periwinkle-colored puffy coat, always remarked how slick it was, how it contoured his body, fit snug. European, cool. "Super warm, too," he said to me one time, as I ran my hand down the shoulder of it.

I am sure that I had more than an inkling of what was about to transpire with my father. Maybe some cliché sense of *carpe diem* took hold of me, as I browned beef and added a four-alarm spice blend to the pot, the air suddenly thick with cumin and coriander and cayenne, spices with their own chromatic spectrum, their own heat and climate. I was briefly in Mexico, the sun furiously life-affirming, the Pacific dazzling, bathed in gold.

Or maybe I wanted the jacket for caution, emergency, to be robed in a color—let's face it—designed to be seen in hostile conditions, to stand out for rescue parties high in forbidding peaks, a color most noticeable in fields of pure white. Titanium White. A high-alert color. A color of tragedy, at least one in the making. Or maybe it was just flat-out impulsive shopping.

Whatever it was, I called her back.

An analysis by web-based Fivethirtyeight, which covered 381 episodes of Bob Ross's iconic series *The Joy of Painting,* found that 91 percent of his canvases contained at least one tree, 44 percent included clouds, 39 percent mountains, and 34 percent mountain lakes. Which all makes sense, particularly considering Ross's military service. Stationed at Fort Eielson, outside Fairbanks, Alaska, that south-Florida son of a Cherokee carpenter saw for the first time the sublime and rugged natural world that would become his painterly obsession. It was also the first time he saw snow.

Yet despite the rigidity of life on a military base, the guy was all serene nature and calm, characteristics he shared with my father: Sierra Club member, outdoor enthusiast, lover of the backpack and metal canteen. (When I came across that canteen after my father died, I could not bear it. I left it there, for the estate-sale people.) I remember as a boy the thrill of hiking my first ten-thousand-foot peak with him, and the long descent during which I could not stop talking, while he calmly listened, contemplative but also relishing—I think now—the satisfaction of having turned me into somewhat of a naturalist.

My father's was a careful, quiet, passive strength. I would say something close to Taoist, even: that soft, abiding reverence for the natural world. He would not, however, have known (let alone self-applied) such a term. Still, when I recall those hikes through Ice House Canyon and into the San Gabriels, up Mount Baldy and Cucamonga Peak, I summon perpetual November: cold but bracingly so; flurries and viscous creek water. I have photos, too, to prove it: lazy, meandering scenes of early winter, steep shadows in ravines, pines shagged with ice, glossy boulders and the occasional, still-resinous, fallen tree. Going nowhere in particular, all day long.

Going nowhere was probably what Ross did, too, in Alaska, at the margins of the known, the entire military base a remnant from the Cold War. Still in that frozen isolation, Ross developed into a formidable quick-paint artist, using a technique originating in Italy called *alla prima,* requiring a fresco-style application of oil-based paints to a washed canvas. (*Wet on wet* is often the English-language analog.)

Skip ahead a decade or so, when the revenue from painting surpassed his military salary, and he resigned, carrying the grandeur and awe of that wild Alaskan terrain, along with its gauzy winter light and his ability to capture it, back to Florida, the Sunshine State. That former Master Sergeant—who made a living out of yelling at boys, yelling at them at the edge of the Arctic Circle, at the end of the world—swore he'd never raise his voice again. And he didn't. Not once. At least not in the videos. Just as I do not ever recall hearing my father raise his. Quiet, passive strength.

I remember once, in the house my wife and I had recently bought, my father was swapping out old face plates on light switches. He asked me, suddenly thrilled to have remembered this small lesson in order, if I knew how to recognize the work of a real union electrician. He pointed to the tiny set-screw in the center of the plate.

"A professional," he said, "always leaves that groove straight up and down."

Bob Ross, born in the Sunshine State in 1942, one year after my father's birth in the Golden State. Opposite ends of the nation; opposite sorts of careers—Ross in the military and art; my father in engineering. The same calming influence. The same reassuring voice. The same amazement at nature. Similar golden boys.

Golden. Like the effect of that entire hipster-coffeehouse, craft-cocktail, upscale dive-bar in Denton, Texas. Pleasantness, warmth. People talking, carrying on. Behind orange curtains (Yellow Ochre, Bright Red, for sure) tied primly, curiously at the waist, the windows frosted over. I didn't want to leave. Maybe my brother's fondness for it. (He had ricocheted around various competitors in town over the years but had lately given himself fully to Golden Boy.) Maybe just the simple warmth of the new jacket—it really *was* warm, and lightweight, and fancy pants— or whatever we might call the heat of keeping busy to ward off grief. Whatever we call it, the three of us were hard at it.

And the place itself helped us, aided us, almost gave off an aura. It hummed with electricity and caffeine and a species of kitsch sharpened to a point far finer than frivolousness. Kitsch with an ineluctable rightness, aptness: honey bees, as if from gold leaf, relieved from the matte-finish, black walls; vintage bulbs pendant and englobed in fish bowls, their filaments glowing golden; golden wingback chairs studiously ironized; golden espresso machine on the counter hulking; golden unicorn tchotchke next to the Golden Boy mug and Golden Boy thermos. Golden: all of it, even our being there, even my writing about it now.

Who else, really, could have been playing on that television? Seems almost obvious, Ross's smile and sunsets spreading over all those blank Alaska days, the cold outside mitigated by the warmth such strokes created. A little heat was all. It's what I thought as I unzipped the hoodie my sister had bought for me. The whole ordeal—the phone call from her ("stuff's so cheap"), her buying the hoodie per my request, our father's death, that moment in the coffeehouse—it all took two months. Tragedies have happened in much less time. They usually do. This was almost worse. It was like survival. It was blizzard conditions. It was avalanche season.

And yet there I was in that hoodie I had worried about, fretted over, my misgivings about the purchase ultimately misplaced. I see that now.

Projected sadness, anticipated remorse, forecasted doubt and uncertainty. "Don't worry," my sister had said on the phone from the Columbia store in October. "If you don't like it, I'll take it back." She had some scheme, anyway. Said she could return later without the special pass, provided she had something to exchange. "I'm buying things I know I'll take back," she said. "Don't worry."

I had, however, become adept at worrying. I treated its maintenance like my running: different forms of punishment, various kinds of senseless pain. I was dumb for running long distances, arguably reckless and impetuous for having my sister buy the hoodie (which, even cheap, wasn't cheap). What was I in the face of my father's death?

I recently read about avalanche science, all the names for the various snow types and minute descriptions that defy such visual, monotonous sameness. To most anyone, snow is snow. It's all the same. Not so for those who study catastrophe. For them, ice crystals can become "hollow" and "cup-shaped," or form "slabs" both "soft" and "hard," or—worse yet—"non-slabs," which create a phenomenon called "pinwheeling," a sure sign of imminent avalanche.

The worst kind of snow, though, at least from an avalanche-prevention standpoint, is "depth hoar." The scientist profiled in the piece called it "the eeriest stuff on any mountain." It rots from the bottom up, vaporizes from ground heat, and causes the top layers to slide away or shear off.

Whole mountainsides. Villages buried. The weight of all that white.

In Chinese, there's a precise word for the blue-gray of distant mountains, a washed-out color specifically defined.

And then there's the other kind of word, one like *golden*, freighted with all the positivity and optimism and richness and beauty only the undying or rich can afford. The Gilded Age. Gold leaf tweezered atop saffron risottos in the poshest ten-table trattorias of Milan. Decadent and Old World.

Golden, though, is a difficult happiness. A happiness with memory, *in* memory, *in memoriam.* For gold always seems slightly elegiac, too. Toppled dynasties, sacked empires, lost paradises. Golden. Nostalgia, too, is always cast in such aureate hues. Maybe that's why my brother and I first started watching *The Joy of Painting:* because joy itself is charged with retro feeling, comes as kitsch or irony (*Oh, joy!*) or as transportation back to some gilded age, some time before worry and ache. Before the end. Maybe that's why I stopped fretting about the jacket.

And it didn't matter that very few of Ross's paintings featured human dwellings. (Fivethirtyeight says 22 percent.) It didn't matter that in the scant episodes in which he did deign to paint a man-made structure—some shack or cabin in the woods—no smoke rose languidly from its chimney, no lamplight burned inside its frosted panes. (In Bob Ross paintings, nobody is ever home.) It didn't matter. Like the great masters of the Far East, the natural world in Ross's paintings dwarfed the human, swallowed it whole or engulfed it. Think Hokusai's terrible waves or the delicate scroll paintings of the Wu School, during China's Ming Dynasty. If there are humans in the scene, they are tiny afterthoughts, useful only for scale.

What mattered was the quality of light. That's what my sister and brother and I said after we left Golden Boy, returned to my father's house. What we thought as we shuffled that night through old slide images of our father as a teenager, his slick hair and lean face, his wry smile. We were mourning, for sure, obsessing over the loss, binging on memory. That flat, midcentury sunlight, at least what the camera captured, worked like a balm. In a series of slides dating to the late '50s, my father is shirtless, in a gleaming white boat, holding a pair of skis. His right hand drapes over them. His left rests on his legs. *Lake Havasu, Arizona,* the back of the slide-box says.

He spoke often of those trips to a cabin owned by his neighbors, how all the local kids descended there in summer for waterskiing and general mayhem. In a mythic story he loved to tell, he was one of five skiers behind the neighbor's boat. They had to incorporate two of the five from another craft, towed separately at first, since the primary boat could not pull five out of the water together. The logistics of it all, I mean. A feat of engineering. At least my father must have thought that, as pleased with the dynamics, the physics, the planning, as he was with the sensation. The golden age of, well, *age.*

In that photo of him in the boat, the sunlight slants, hits his face from the left, stipples the water in white. I'd say Titanium White, but it's tinnier, realer, more immediate. It's actual sunlight, preserved, as he is, on film. And I keep coming back to it.

And he's so damn happy, he's glowing.

Unsent Letter to the Living #3

Dear XXXXX,

Though I missed you at my father's service, I understand. We all have our commitments and our small Igloo coolers, our stacks of seldom-watched DVDs tucked in the drawer of an old entertainment system, even our own cookware. That is why it struck me as odd, your calling me a week or so after the memorial, at night—must have been around 10:00 p.m.—to inquire about a few things you had left at my father's house during your last visit to see him a month or so prior.

He was gravely ill by then, even if we all pretended he wasn't, so the fact that he didn't return your CorningWare, in which I can only assume you delivered some sort of sturdy, starchy casserole (*hearty,* we call it, for some unexplained reason) in a small Igloo cooler, or the DVD—the title of which you curiously omitted in our conversation— the fact that he didn't return these things before his death should not strike you as odd.

Even you admitted that asking for those quotidian artifacts—terrestrial, residual, commonplace—might strike me as a bit odd, which it did, so odd in fact that I really had no answer for you.

So much of this process of my father's death, I find, is strikingly unanswerable, unexplainable, hopelessly provisional, full of holes and fissures.

Just today, for example, while driving what used to be his car—a car older than my brother or my sister or I, a car I had shipped four states away in order that I might still hear the sound of that engine, a sound I heard throughout my childhood as my father downshifted into second, rolled into my adolescence—I noticed a small, black toggle switch underneath the steering column. Though he must have installed it, I have no idea what the switch is for, as I assume you do not. And I have nobody to ask who might explain.

That switch might as well be some cipher, a sign, a key to unlocking some inscrutable language of loss, a language similar to the one you deployed when speaking with me on the phone a week or so after my father's service. Sure, it *sounded* like English, replicated its cadences, the vocabulary strikingly similar. It's just that when you admitted how odd it must sound—your asking for those replaceable, humdrum, material conveniences: a dish, a cooler, a DVD—we would soon be holding my father's ashes in a small, cooler-size urn, and would watch as a delightful man originally from England but currently the caretaker (I love that term) of the small cemetery where my father was soon to be buried, watch as he carefully (tastefully, almost) set the urn in the ground, then filled the hole with dirt, gently patted it down.

I forgot to say that the caretaker didn't even keep the shovel in view; that he took care to conceal it, while we stood graveside; that, when the time came, he had to go around a nearby tree to fetch it, the sight of it, perhaps, in his mind, too earthly, too real for that unreal experience we were experiencing, my sister, my brother, and I, while my brother's daughter—whose name is Clara, named after my grandmother, a name that means *clear* or *bright*—while she fidgeted, clearly uncomfortable with the entire scene, which is what we were, too, *uncomfortable,* struck by the odd clarity of the day—crisp January afternoon, trees shivering over those hoary stones—the air buoyant, almost lifting us—while all the movements of the caretaker tended down, toward the ground, which was so hard, he told us, that the machines had struggled to tear a hole in it.

Still, the care he took with us: do you understand what I'm saying?

Yes, even you admitted that asking for a glass baking dish—let alone a plastic cooler and a DVD (*Dirty Dancing*? A documentary on rainforests?)—that it might strike me as odd, strike me as a shovel might a shin; and so I waited for the rationale, the explanation. While I waited,

I may have even recalled the etymology of *explanation—an unfolding—* which originally carried that sense of *opening out,* as might the bud of a fantastic flower. I must have imagined your rationale, then, opening out, blossoming into delicate paeans to a grandmother long since departed, who cooked casseroles for you in *that particular* CorningWare dish; the transplant organ for your beloved niece transported—oddly enough—in *that precise* Igloo cooler; *that one copy* of *that one* DVD a keepsake from your mother, a massive Patrick Swayze fan who often warmed herself by his bright biceps and rhythmic heat.

Any of those reasons would have struck me as reasonable, as reasons go. Reasonable in the way the caretaker looked at the urn that carried my father's ashes and—without acting put out or annoyed—simply told us that it was a bit larger than usual, that he might, as he put it, "have to make some last-minute adjustments." Reasonable, too, when he was correct, when it didn't quite fit.

Reasonable as we were, my brother, my sister, and I—when we allowed him some privacy, some time alone with the shovel and the cold earth, that he might take care to render our father's descent and our witnessing of it a little less excruciating.

Striking, how none of us wished to hear the striking of his shovel.

It struck me just today that wherever your CorningWare dish is now, post-estate-sale, whither your DVD has journeyed, and whose Diet Cokes your Igloo cooler now harbors: these are questions as unanswerable as death itself. You might as well ask where we all go once the dance is over and the music stops.

For my father, I imagine a place much like that resort in *Dirty Dancing:* somewhere intensely upstate, with rocking chairs on a wide veranda overlooking a lake, a place eternally caught in the sticky, amber light of late summer, '50s music lost then rediscovered daily. I forget the name of that fictitious place in the film, but then I forget lots of little things like that, lots of tiny, inconsequential things. Loads of them, in fact, by the tonnage: phone numbers of former colleagues, the recipe for that deeply earthy enchilada sauce, the whereabouts of any one glass dish or small cooler. Gwen and I, we have three or four such coolers, and I don't remember even buying one. They simply accumulate, like snow.

Besides, it's finally unverifiable, unclear, this concept of hell as all flames and heat and such. Dante's version, for example, suggests that the worst parts—those regions reserved for the most craven sinners, the folks with ice in their blood—the worst parts are frigid; and that Satan—Old Scratch himself, his great wings spread and striking the air—remains half-buried in the underworld's frozen core, stuck, driven deep into the ice after God struck him down for his transgressions, which had to do with wanting something he couldn't (he shouldn't) have back.

Sincerely,
Chad

My Amontillado

This is a story about wine or, rather, "wine by number," as my friend called it, when I explained to him my plan to make the stuff. "We could do this," I said, speaking of the wine kits I had studied: concentrates in prepackaged amounts, along with the yeast, the sulfides for sanitation, the sorbates for preservation, chitosan for clarification ("fining," in the jargon), sometimes even bottle labels with lots of cursive fonts and words like *estate* and *primeur cru* and *chateau this-and-that* and other Frenchy things.

Over three years working together at the university, we had become close friends, Gwen and I, he and his wife. We sat often on the porch of their Craftsman house, groused about work, listened to music, and drank too much.

"I'm sick of paying fifteen bucks for grocery-store swill," I said.

After an initial investment in gear (not more than $200), I argued that we could make a $3 bottle. He emptied some Sauvignon Blanc into our glasses.

"I'm in," he said.

That next weekend, we drove to a home-brewing store in Atlanta and loaded up.

A sense of industry, of savings, I'm sure, was partly at play, as was the forging of a new friendship, one full of projects, of collaborations, and a fair amount of sitting around drinking. We shared a love of music and travel and food and good things; things that invite expertise, knowledge, classification.

And where we differed, we soon blended. He got me into gardening, helped me rototill, taught me which tomatoes to plant, what to do about slugs, watered our small plot when we went away for a weekend. I admired his apparent selflessness, the zeal with which he rushed to help me, to help students, to take cans to the soup kitchen.

I got him into cycling, and we quickly took to the backroads of rural Georgia, chatty about a future that, at least in those early days, felt expansive and cavernous, a space we could inhabit together, enjoying the better parts of that small quasi-college-town, with its cheap housing, great cycling, and dinner parties with copious amounts of irony and alcohol.

Making wine, though, was about more than simple industry or friendship. Making wine also allowed me to act out my own Italian fantasy, to approximate some Old World myth of the noble peasant, the thought of making wine perhaps even more intoxicating than consuming it. Homemade wine was inextricably tied in my mind to my friend Dino and his cellar in Bologna: those rows of anonymous, identical, fat-bottomed, green bottles, alongside fifty-liter demijohns in wicker cradles; last weekend's cache of porcini in a small, wooden crate; jars and jars of tomatoes on a vinyl-covered table stacked with excess dishes. Arriving for dinner, as I had done dozens of times during my twenties, I often asked for the keys, volunteered to fetch the wine.

Dino didn't tend his own vines, I should say, but instead took those demijohns (massive glass carboys) down to the local wine consortium every so often, and bought the stuff wholesale. When he returned, he and a few friends would sit around the cellar with a siphon and some clean bottles—along with a healthy length of sausage, a wedge of cheese, a free Saturday afternoon—and bottle enough wine for the season.

Odd desire: that wish of twenty-four-year-old me to sit with a group of older Italian men bottling wine, gnawing on sausage, telling dirty jokes. I romanticized it all: that sense of wine uncoupled from capitalism, from exercises of class; that vaguely illicit feel of moonshining, of a kind of alchemy grafted onto Italian ease and homespun camaraderie.

It's what I imagined, too, as we started our own wine production, my friend and I. To finish the fantasy, though, we needed a designated place. We needed a wine cellar.

☻

What I had was an eight-by-twelve-foot cinder-block box, the substructure of our house's old porch, which was extended and enclosed to make way for a sunroom overhead, all before Gwen and I moved in. One must first pass through the area underneath that sunroom, a workshop of sorts, then up a small step and through a latched door in the back, to enter the wine cellar.

It was hardly a wine cellar at all, hardly the cavernous vaults of Montresor's Palace in Poe's "The Cask of Amontillado," wherein the famed vintage supposedly lies, where Montresor bids come his erstwhile friend Fortunato. Like Poe's creepy vaults, though, my cellar was its own sort of boneyard, a place where paint cans had gone to die, where rusty saw blades and chicken-wire bundles gathered near boxes of now-banned pesticides and noxious, plastic-melting potions meant to kill or maim, where all that moldered in the dark, under layers of hoar and amnesia.

"Yikes," my friend said, when I took him on a tour and suggested that it might be a perfect place for a wine cellar. "Perfect place for a horror flick," he said.

And he was right, at least until my father helped me clear the space long ago. We built shelving, even ran water to it. (The sink was taken from his house, detritus from a kitchen remodel.) I never could, however, clear the smell completely, not one of synthetic chemicals so much as something older, deeper, more archetypal. Montresor refers to it as "nitre" (or potassium nitrate), which webs the walls of the dank caverns beneath his family's palace.

The smell of age, of the subterranean, of the eerie, the underworld.

I'm sure there was more than a bit of class-consciousness, too, in my wanting to produce wine in the first place, to keep it all in a cellar. Mine was a bifurcated symbolism of wine: at once outside class but also—lurking in my visions of a spiral staircase down to the cellar from our sunroom (a staircase I never built)—deeply supportive of class, aspirational and freighted. Those first few batches we made I approached with much enthusiasm, checking on the wine obsessively during the month-long process, presiding over the incremental steps with the smug, self-congratulating joy of a lord over his horse stables.

●

Everything went as planned. French Sauvignon Blancs and Australian Chardonnays highly drinkable and, yes, three dollars per. My friend loved it, in particular the bottling stage, when he would leave with case after case. We told everyone that we were making our own wine, as proud of our accomplishment as we were of our partnership, our team.

Poe's tale, too, is somewhat about a wine-based friendship, albeit one gone . . . sour. A bad pun, I know, yet one befitting Poe, whose names in "The Cask of Amontillado" carry a similar hamfistedness: Montresor ("My treasure") exuding that faded aura of nobility; Fortunato ("The fortunate one"), some nouveau-riche player trying to buy himself class with—at least in Montresor's final estimation—no class at all.

We never really know why Montresor has decided to condemn his friend to death in the cellar vaults. We can only glean that Fortunato overstepped his boundaries, his drunkenness suspect from the beginning, as was his "motley" style of dress and poor taste. "In painting and gemmary," adds Montresor, "Fortunato, like his countrymen, was a quack." One senses that the problem with Fortunato, at least in the eyes of Montresor, is simply that he had either not quite earned his right to be a noble or, worse, had tried too hard.

My friend and I, though, fancied ourselves fancier, at least more worldly. Once, in what turned out to be the middle days of our friendship, we met up in Italy, he and his wife visiting for a week. I was teaching on a study-abroad program in wine-crazed Montepulciano, with a fabulous apartment, a rooftop terrace. We climbed to its withered wooden table each evening, a chilled bottle in hand, and watched the swifts dart and dive. Having him with me, in Italy, the place I had grown to love, around the language and food and wine for which I had culti-vated a deep appreciation: it was like inducting him into my family. We were entering a new phase of our friendship, one which would develop its own architecture, provide a foundation on which to combine our independent lives.

☻

Wine was with us all the time. Wine in our crawl space and in a Tuscan hilltop town. Wine as catalyst, as talking point, as measure of our in-telligence and sophistication. Wine as pleasure and refreshment and intoxicating joy. Wine as ominous elixir, though, as excuse and cover, crutch and cloak. It's what Poe romanticizes, too, I think, from a safe, fictional distance—that emphasis on wine as symbol, as capital, as cul-tural marker, yes, but also as weakness and vice, as vainglorious posture and imminent threat.

And while the Montresor catacombs are a far cry from Dino's cellar stash or my spruced-up crawl space, still I'd be lying if I didn't sense a bit of that nobility each time I appraised my wine rack: dust settling on the necks of bottles in repose there, caught in the beam of my flashlight or, even better, the light of torches, of "flambeaux," in Poe's fittingly pained Euro-nostalgia. "Flambeaux," which the devilish Montresor slides from their sconces—one for himself, the other for inebriated Fortunato—as they descend through the vaults, on the hunt for the rare Amontillado.

We had our aspirations, too, my friend and I. An early kit—a Brunello, one of the prized Italian varietals—cost us almost twice the regular amount. A more complicated process ensued, involving much more juice (and less addition of water) along with a Mylar bag of grape skins for extra tannin and color extraction, oak chips to simulate the cask. This was to be our opus, I thought, our coup, our hack, our own Amontillado.

When we were done, we could barely stand the wait. One month, two, three. When we finally sampled it after four months, however, we were less than impressed. The wine carried a faintly herbaceous after-taste, as if we had thrown a handful of rosemary into the vat. "Tastes like sadness," I said, realizing that we couldn't hack our way into the expensive stuff. We couldn't fake it.

My friend tried to spin it all, thinking maybe the wine would improve with age. He was the eternal optimist when it came to making wine, and with good reason: he drank a lot of it. When we bottled a kit (each one yielding just under thirty bottles), he was gleeful, buzzing with talk of what we could do, seriously do, together. He was overexcited in the way—I later realized—an addict behaves around an abundance of his chosen vice. A week or two later, though, when we visited for dinner or sat on their porch, he'd bring out some commercial wine. When I raised an eyebrow, he'd shrug somewhat sheepishly. "We kind of burned through ours already."

"I perceive you are afflicted," Montresor says to the drunken Fortunato, as they descend into the earth. I wonder how the dandy didn't see what was coming. I wonder how I didn't either: the way my friend would often drink to the point of slurring his speech; how, as we chatted late into the night on the porch, he would slowly start to nod off, a glass of wine tipping in his hand; how his eyes—just as Poe describes those of Fortunato—resembled "two filmy orbs that distilled the rheum of intoxication."

Once, near the end of a bike ride, he asked if I ever experienced intense, cold sweats while we cycled. "No," I said adamantly, a bit confused by the question. Only much later did I realize he was probably feeling the after-effects of too much drinking, riding on a hangover, DTs at twenty miles per hour. Often, while sharing a bottle on the porch, we would agree to meet at his place for a ride the next morning; yet he would not appear, even after I called, banged on his backdoor. We were friends, though, and friends did not point out the weaknesses of friends. Friends did not fret over their friends' indulgences, particularly when those indulgences aided a mutual obsession.

Besides, that week in Montepulciano also set the stage for him to help me start our university's program in Italy, which he was more than happy to do. I'd perform most of the work: setting it up, making contacts with private language schools, housing agents, transportation companies. He'd provide moral support and companionship, my copilot, my cheerleader.

He tried desperately to inhabit that role, too. He labored at the language, at the culture, at everything. He badly wanted to participate in much more than simply shepherding students through Italy's wonders, wanted to be more than simply the guy fortunate to have a friend with connections. I can admit, too, that there was a power dynamic, as there almost naturally is, between two people in a foreign country, when one of them (me) speaks the language at least well enough to conduct business and get what he wants, while the other (my friend) defers.

As we grew more confident, more gluttonous in production and consumption, I even enticed my friend to make an effervescent, dry red wine, like the Lambrusco I loved in Bologna. No Amontillado, no, but if my friend were going to help me live a kind of Italian fantasy, which I had kept deep within my sense of self all those years, he had to say yes.

Since Lambrusco was not available in kits, my friend even did most of the research on how to approximate it, reading posts on obscure home-brewing sites, deep diving into rogue vintner manuals. To summarize: in order to achieve the wine's effervescence, we mixed a bit of sugar syrup into the vat at the tail end of its first fermentation, while omitting the sulfides to kill any remaining yeast. Instead what little that remained alive through transfer would begin to digest the additional sugar, the byproduct of which is carbon dioxide, or fizz. And instead of siphoning it all into large glass carboys, the wine and remaining yeast went straight into stout-sided Champagne bottles able to withstand the increased pressure.

To our amazement our first trials went smoothly, producing a fizzy, dry red. Not Lambrusco precisely but delicious all the same. To think: Dino's wine, not in Bologna but right here, in my cellar, in a quasi-college-town in Georgia. "We will have many a rich laugh about it," Fortunato claims of their foray into the vaults. To the very end, that need for friendship, for belonging.

And I encouraged it all: the purchasing of two more primary fermenters (glorified, six-gallon paint buckets with airtight lids), the increased production, the hoarding of bottles and asking of friends for empties, hitting up the local bar for their trash on a Monday.

I made a crude, wall-sized, 150-bottle wine rack and dreamed of stacking vintage wines, awaiting the ideal night, the perfectly paired meal, the impressive guest list. The rack, however, never filled. The more we made, it seemed, the more we drank, my friend especially. I began to watch during our bottling sessions, ensuring that he didn't take more than his share. Sometimes he'd ask for a loan of sorts, an advance of ten bottles from my stash. "Are we bottling this weekend?" he'd message to ask. "We're all out, over here."

Pressure and time are all it took to make fizzy wine, but really not much time at all. "From bucket to gullet," my friend would say, "in just over three weeks." Since we were no longer following the kit's explicit instructions, however, we also had our mishaps. In some batches, the fizz wouldn't take. (Not enough live yeast remained from the first fermentation.)

More often, though, we produced shockingly effervescent bottles, which we had to chill completely before opening, else risk a volcanic eruption upon snipping the wire cage that (just barely) held the cork in place. We became sensitive to bottles that seemed under extreme duress, could recognize the corks pushing, straining at their wire cages: all that pressure building, with nowhere to go. The websites and rebel winemakers online had warned us, too. "Wear protective gear," they said, "goggles and thick aprons." They offered dire pronouncements. "Don't mess around with fizzy wine."

Once, after a few weeks' absence, we entered the cellar to find the concrete ceiling splattered in red, like a murder scene. A bottle had exploded with such apparent force that the biggest piece of glass we found was the intact, round base of the bottle itself, still sitting on the shelf, in line with the other bottles. Otherwise, the thing had transformed into shards at high velocity, into shrapnel, a jagged piece of which had lodged into the shelving. We left it there as a reminder, a *memento mori,* an omen.

☠

"I took from their sconces two flambeaux," Montresor recounts, "and giving one to Fortunato, bowed him through several suites of rooms to the archway that led into the vaults." I passed to my friend a license to overdrink, not just in our cellar, out of the Apollonian glare, but also in Italy, where we scheduled our days—away from our wives for the month—around late afternoon spritzes, wine lists at dinner, postprandial bitters. We weren't alcoholics, mind you, particularly when we labored to know, *really know,* the products, the local varietals, the *terroir.* We weren't alcoholics if we told ourselves so. We bowed each other through the archways of Italy.

There were scrapes, though, points at which I should have intervened. Once, with some Italian friends at a villa in the countryside, on a walk down a dirt road under a canopy of stars, I noticed he was gripping by the neck a Prosecco bottle taken from the dinner table. He was slurring his speech, stumbling along. "Is your friend okay?" one of the Italians whispered to me, clearly aghast. In a country drenched in wine, odd how overdrinking is so much maligned. I was mortified, made excuses, resented him all the next day.

Or at dinner, at our program's partner-restaurant, where we brought all the students each weeknight, he grew comfortable helping himself to more of their tap wine. One of the food servers—a friend by then, too—would give him a raised eyebrow every time and say half-jokingly (which means half-seriously), "Hey, look at the drunk go!"

By most any metric, he *was* a drunk. He would sleep through early meetings on which we had agreed. He would appear as if an apparition yet stinking of booze, just as the train pulled in the station for a planned trip with the students.

"I took from their sconces two flambeaux," Montresor says. He is leading Fortunato down, but Fortunato takes the torch. Fortunato wants the famed Amontillado.

One summer, the final summer of our Italian partnership, of our friendship, he started an affair with a woman he met through the language school in town. His wife—my close friend, too—wrote to me halfway through our program. "I hate to ask," she wrote, "but what is going on with him and that woman?" She had seen photos online, she said, heard tell of this "friend." I was blind, I think now, to the obvious intrigue, the obviousness in general, the stink of booze, his footfalls in the stairwell between our two rental apartments, late, late at night.

I played it off, thought unlikely any romance between them, saw my friend instead capitalizing on the woman's newness to the town (she, a foreigner like him), a chance to show off his growing knowledge, act the expert, away from me. But even that did not explain his augmented mania, by then manifested in unstoppable monologues over drinks, at dinner, late at night; his constant, nervous chatter; the sheer amounts of wine. "For the love of God, Montresor!"

One morning I stopped him in the middle of one of his laborious narratives—a rambling excuse for why he had not woken up in time. I told him finally to stop, to shut up. I hugged him (not something we did much), said I loved him (not something we did ever), but that he was out of control.

"You're right," he said, "I know."

He calmed down, claimed that his wife was worried too, said he had stopped taking his medication (for bipolar disorder or depression or anxiety; I never really knew but never really asked).

"Now you know," he said, "what Bizarro-me looks like."

"It was about dusk," Montresor says, "one evening during the supreme madness of the carnival season, that I encountered my friend." That last summer, too, felt almost always dusk, as my friend and our friendship both disintegrated in Italy, land of my obsessions. "The nitre!" Montresor exclaims to Fortunato. "It hangs like moss upon the vaults. We are below the river's bed." He has brought Fortunato there to wall him in, to silence him forever. "The drops of moisture trickle among the bones."

I, too, had grown cold (at best), perhaps full of schadenfreude (at worst). I had tried on three occasions to reach my friend, to help steer him away from the end for which he seemed headed. Still he kept up his mania, his carnivalesque absurdity, trying desperately—it seemed—to prove he was not going mad. The more he tried to persuade, however, the more manic his attempts became.

I began to ignore him, cut out early, claim to be tired. I still had no idea (didn't *want* to have the idea) that he was involved with another woman. "I passed down a long and winding staircase," Montresor continues, "requesting him to be cautious as he followed." Montresor is leading Fortunato to his doom, counting on his friend's weakness for showing off, his gluttonous need for wine, yes, but also for attention, recognition, approval, belonging.

Had I somehow pushed my friend to seek acceptance elsewhere? Was my rejection of his behavior the catalyst or just some ragged consequence?

"We came at length to the foot of the descent, and stood together on the damp ground of the catacombs."

Was I his Montresor? Had I—however unwittingly—encouraged or at least allowed my friend to walk toward his own terrible demise? Who was leading whom?

That summer in which my friend became someone else entirely, I did, too. I had no response, finally, when he lashed out, accusing me of wrongdoings I was scarcely able to imagine, let alone assume blame for. Back home, there were attempts by him to patch it up, concessions to temporary insanity, late-night confessions to our mutual friends, which always somehow cast guilt back on me. "The guy is hurting," one friend told me. "He's got you wrapped up in all sorts of other trauma." Family deaths and abandonment, a verifiable history of alcohol abuse, instability. I was being led down into my friend's concealed past, descending into the psyche of a person I thought I knew.

There were also drunken screeds, messages sent to me in haste, violent and untethered, in which I was blamed for my callousness in the hilltop towns of Umbria. I, some Fortunato, presented with my inventory of faults, led by flambeaux into the labyrinth.

Finally, I had to shut it all off, extinguish the friendship, foreclose any future. He was lost to me, as he was to his former wife, to whom he left that Craftsman house, itself a Poe-like presence by then, a House of Usher. I helped her clean the rotten shed. I carted rusty garden tools to the dump.

One must first pass through the area underneath our sunroom, a workshop of sorts, then up a small step and through a latched door in the back, to enter the wine cellar. Back, back into the bowels of the house. Back into history now, I can still replay the scenes at dinner in Italy that summer, when my friend ceased to be my friend, as he poured, with a shaky hand, another stout glass from the carafe. I finally looked upon him as a stranger, since I had by then departed the province of compassion, the kingdom of friendship. I looked upon him as if he were already a ghost, a non-entity, an embarrassment to the noble house of my Italian fantasy.

We never really understand, it's true, just how Fortunato has offended Montresor. All we know is that—at least in the eyes of the aristocrat—it happened. My friend detonated a friendship and a marriage that summer. The marriage probably should have ended sooner but required a rogue to overstep. The friendship? I wish that were still intact. In that respect, my friend was both Montresor *and* Fortunato, executioner and condemned alike. I watched as he walled himself in, his wife and me out.

Part of me, though, thinks that *I* was Fortunato, passing for Italian with my pressed shirts and friends in local bars, my knowledge of the local cultivars. I cringed that summer not so much at my friend's growing drunkenness and pathological lying (no affair, he swore, no disintegrating marriage, no late-night benders) as much as his embarrassing me in my adopted country. He was unwittingly calling me out for who I was: forger, fiction, gamer, fake.

For half a century, Montresor concludes at the end of "The Cask of Amontillado," his friend's bones lay behind the catacomb wall. "No mortal has disturbed them," he says. "In pace requiescat!" And yet, is not Montresor, in his retelling of his crime, disturbing the very bones he insists lie still? Is he not agitating the peace he takes credit for preserving?

Nearing the completion of his labor, Montresor even gestures at a kind of regret, mentioning that his "heart grew sick." He has just walled Fortunato into the vaults of his palace. And even if he blames such feelings on "the dampness of the catacombs," we easily see through such talk. I do, at least. It is Montresor who is consigned to his own guilt, his own crime, alone in the vaults of his past, monumental and dark, webbed with nitre.

One must first pass through the origins of my friendship before descending into the vaults of that terrible summer, in which my friend became someone else entirely. I have shown you those vaults now, the construction of our friendship, and the camaraderie and obsessions therein.

I have shown you Italy, too, at least the version we created for ourselves back then, two friends amid those fantastic ruins, drinking it all in.

The Puzzle

"You'll never guess what I'm doing," my sister said over the phone. Her kids were away at college. It was too late in the evening for her to garden or run. "I'm doing a puzzle."

And, no, I never would have guessed that, since my family is not a puzzle family. Not like Gwen's family, who, every summer, during our weeklong vacation together, sets out to finish some massive, over-busy puzzle, the choice of which her two sisters fret over for months leading up to the trip. Once on site, they huddle around a table each day—her sisters mainly but also her mother, her nieces and nephews in turn, every once in a while even Gwen and I, even my brothers-in-law—and pick over the pieces.

While I found it all initially a waste of time, I also recognized it as an excuse for them to do nothing, permission to relax, with that notional task set before them, some distant focal point. Yet doing a puzzle, even in some impatient, dressed-up-adolescent way, requires what seems a *narrowing* of the gaze; a scrutinizing of particularities. Microscopic, not macroscopic, vision.

"I don't know why," my sister said, "but I'm addicted to this thing." She talked about the colors of the puzzle she was then working on—its hypnotic blues and oranges—and the image itself, by a contemporary artist, featuring bluebirds in a simplified orange orchard.

"It's the warmth," she said, a bit breathless, really, talking about how, after a while, her eyes could instantly detect slight variations in the values of color, differentiate between *this* orange and *that* orange, *this* bird and *that* bird. (From a distance, she said, they all looked the same.)

"And the pieces," she continued, "they fit together perfectly." This was no discount knock-off. This was a *real* puzzle, whatever that meant.

A few days later, old friends posted a photo of themselves and their two grown daughters leaning over a table, van Gogh's *The Starry Night* jigsawed into tiny pieces under them. "Family-night puzzle," the caption said.

What the hell, I remember thinking to myself. *Maybe I should do a puzzle.*

☻

In my puzzle of Edward Hopper's 1929 painting *Chop Suey,* two women sit at lunch together, independent, enjoying the sunlight, which streams through the windows of that affordable, unsophisticated restaurant. It's the second story, after all; and it's Chinese food or, rather, *Americanized* Chinese food, which lends to the interior a humble feel. This is no fine dining establishment. The spare décor and cheap window designs attest to that. No trap of convention, though, either. These women are at least there of their own volition.

While the majority of the puzzle pieces, pushed to one side of my table, form a menacing field of grainy blacks and gray-browns, the women in their flapper caps and modestly colored clothing provide a measured counterpoint. One sports a striped scarf—bright blue and yellow and white silk—around a gray-blue cardigan of sorts; the other—the woman facing me—a fine cashmere sweater of green (it *is* cashmere, at least the rendering of it in paint), bright red lipstick, a glint catching in her azure earrings.

And even if she (the one with the lipstick, the bright earrings, which echo her blue eyes), even if she is less than emotive; and even if she appears to look beyond the shoulder of her friend, as if they were engaged somehow in two different conversations; at least they are two young women enjoying some modicum of independence, away from the stolid conventions and loveless relationship suggested by the reserved couple obscured in the background (almost part of the background). *That* woman stares searchingly at the man (presumably her husband); he peers down at his cigarette.

This painting might just be a bit of an anomaly for Hopper, too, who mostly preferred isolated individuals for his models (almost always women), or couples who seem more isolated from each other, even if the canvas presented them together. (That couple in the shadows of *Chop Suey:* they seem more the Hopper type.)

This painting was a puzzle long before its likeness was jigsawed for me.

Hopper was not, however, the first puzzle I worked on. One puzzle came before, the Ur-puzzle, the beginning. A friend laughed when I told him about it over the phone. "Not you, too," he said. "Everyone's doing puzzles now." And it is true that I had not just stumbled onto the idea by myself, and neither had my sister or friends. And it was not a sickness, really, some contagion spreading the ineluctable need to reassemble fragmented images.

But it *was* a sickness of another kind that brought me at least to the idea of a puzzle, since the world was a week or so into the COVID-19 pandemic, which had shuttered everything and mandated that most of us shelter in place. That's why my sister had somehow arrived at puzzles; that's why my friends and their daughters had, too (no natural van Gogh enthusiasts); and that's why I had thought, *What the hell.*

Might be peaceful, I reasoned, losing myself in a simple task, the pop-culture equivalent of a rock garden, Bonsai for the less patient, a way of turning off the mind without resorting to drugs or booze. Reading the news each morning, the mounting number of cases, the fears of hospitals overwhelmed, markets crashing: I'm sure all of that drove me to seek a kind of purposeful mindlessness—peace, stillness, of any kind—which is what I thought a puzzle might provide.

Peaceful, too, when those bluebirds and oranges arrived (a gift from my sister, after I had expressed my interest in the puzzle she first got hooked on, *her* Ur-puzzle), and I spread the pieces out dutifully, turning each one over, trying to *lose myself* in the process, the minutiae, the simple feel of each piece in my hand. Peaceful, too (mostly), finding all the border pieces—that staple first move of most any puzzle person—until I could not find the final few.

Frustration, then, standing up, leaning over the wooden table, scouring some 960 or so pieces for the one or two still missing. Had my sister dropped some on the floor? Did they fall out when I dumped the box on the table?

More frustrating still, later, with the border accomplished, was all the maddening sameness of those colors. At one point I thought about quitting. Screw it. My sister was a masochist. What a waste of time. Why wasn't I writing or reading or, hell, painting the deck (which badly needed it), taking care of the yard?

I tried to enlist Gwen, tried to make it some lame, quarantine bonding ritual, something we could at least go mad doing together.

"Screw that," she said. "Last thing I want to do."

She reminded me that she got stuck doing those damn things for a week each summer with her family. "That's plenty for me," she said and plopped down on the couch with some budget rosé and a book on upper-back exercises.

Thus the very thing I had hoped would help me relax, aid me in respecting the enormous amounts of time I had on my hands, became instead an instrument of aggravation and, ultimately, guilt. The disembodied eyes of those bluebirds stared at me when I walked by—an emblem of my failure to follow through.

Slowly, though, I started to assign myself small tasks. *Just find ten pieces,* I'd say. *Just look for those few bees* (whose striped bodies rendered them more obvious). "The journey of a thousand miles" I could see on some horrible inspirational poster.

Slowly, however, I *did* give myself over to those well-defined acts of solving the puzzle (*just ten pieces, just the rest of this one orange*). I even started to enjoy the hunt, the eureka moment—the instant recognition, almost preternatural—locating that stray piece, the feel of it clicking into place, even as I *knew* it would, that it *had* to. Soon, in fact, I was portioning out my time, setting limits. It became a slight privilege to sit there with a beer in the evening and pore over the work. I looked forward to it. The challenge became not to do *too much.*

"Honestly," I told my sister one night on the phone, "I don't want it to end."

•

And there was, at least early on, also a part of me that did not want the lockdown to end. All that time, suddenly, to tend to the house, to catch up on reading, to *not engage:* it was a bit intoxicating. I was like a character in a Hopper canvas, awash in some vast isolation but somehow content, relieved. Gwen did not quite know what to do with the time and so took to working out compulsively, cleaning closets, constructing ziggurats of Goodwill donations. I, however, relished an empty day, calendar cleared, as spartan as a Hopper interior.

Having finished the birds and oranges, and with a bit more experience under my belt, I wanted to take even more time with the next one, that one-thousand-piece jigsaw of Hopper's *Chop Suey.* Not as familiar with the painting as with some others, still I imagined that I might find some enjoyment from staring at Hopper's work for a while, assembling the puzzle by myself, piece by piece.

After the border, I sorted all the pieces associated with that cropped *Chop Suey* sign, which I finished in an evening. Next, the blurry window designs (which Hopper created out of muddied reds and dull greens). The question became not so much why I was doing it or when it might end but instead how I might string it along, savor each piece. The puzzle was how to *continue* the puzzle.

And Hopper seemed an ideal candidate for such an exercise. Isolation, I thought: now *that* is something Hopper knew—isolated people, even (perhaps especially) when together with others; evacuated public spaces, eerily lit automats, and shuttered storefronts; the glow of early evening concrete; the crepuscular, static vistas of cityscapes emptied of their people.

On the other hand, what a depressing thought: to think Hopper the perfect puzzle subject for (and of) isolation, the patron saint of loneliness. Why not call it Zen serenity, meaningful solitude, a chance for mindlessness? And why did I have to search for meaning in isolation as seriously as those Hopper figures contemplated their own vacuous lives?

I had a second idea: I would read a Hopper biography while completing the puzzle, and write about it all. And when the biography came—all seven hundred pages of it—and when I started to read (sorry, but it's a tad dull, as Hopper himself—though a fantastic painter—was, as taciturn and distant as that gentlemen in the shadows of *Chop Suey*), the puzzle became complicated by my anxieties about assembling all the information, putting the pieces together—the quarantine, the artist, the biography, the puzzle, my own reasons for doing it—telling the story, whatever story there was to tell.

Here's the story of the painting, at least. The two women—the two I've been describing—as well as the third, whom we only see in shadow, in profile, part of that unhappy couple washed in grainy grays and purple-blues—turns out all those women were modeled on Hopper's wife, Jo. An artist herself, she ended up taking a backseat to Hopper's fame, self-sacrificing, at least from the point of view of the biography, which relies heavily on Jo's meticulous journals and letters.

Jo is everywhere in Hopper's work. As such, she is also the emblem of distance, of a cratered interior life rendered visible, in canvas after canvas. She is everywhere, that is, and nowhere, extant now mostly as Hopper's prop, Hopper's mannequin, replicated again and again as a stand-in for monotony.

She's the same puzzle piece, over and over. And she always fits.

And that location, the chop-suey joint: turns out Hopper probably had in mind a particular place—second story, cheap (he was nothing if not thrifty), on Columbus Circle, south edge of the Upper West Side—

which he and Jo frequented early in their courting and marriage. Was this painting a kind of love letter to Jo? Was Hopper capable of that? ("Sometimes talking with Eddie is just like dropping a stone in a well," Jo wrote in her journal, "except that it doesn't thump when it hits bottom.") Or was the painting a self-conscious admission of his own tendency to push her away, to keep private? (A contemporary, quoted in the biography, maintains that Hopper painted a line down the middle of his studio space, which even his wife dared not cross.)

That woman in the restaurant, the peculiar way she seems both engaged in conversation but also staring into the distance above the shoulder of her friend (if the other woman is even a friend): uncanny, how Hopper—with spare use of detail—depicts with such specificity the psychology of the searching gaze, as if the farther that woman looks into the distance, the more interiorized her vision becomes.

That look on her face, too—the mannequin, the isolate, the artist's own wife—must have been a look Hopper knew intimately. Or one he cultivated in her.

Time softened and blurred. One month, two months. Our cars sat idle in the garage. We grew sensitive to the changing light on the lake outside, spotted infrequent birds more frequently. Nothing too precious or rare but still not birds we see year round: wood ducks nesting again in the tree across the cove; purple martins finally—we swore—setting up shop in the tiny house we erected years ago, a house that had become almost haunted, a miniature Hopper house. (He remained fond his entire life of lonely, Victorian monstrosities like the one he grew up in. Hitchcock is rumored to have taken inspiration for *Psycho* from Hopper's *House by the Railroad*.)

Classes by then complete and grades turned in, random (even some fairly perfunctory) house projects accomplished, still time stretched before us, out across the summer months, where typically we would be in Italy, running a university program, basking in the frenetic, sweltering piazzas of Spoleto, of Rome. This summer, nothing. More than once I caught myself staring out our window to the small lake for an indeterminate amount of time, my gaze relaxing until the entire cove—the water, the maples surrounding it, the houses tucked into the pines beyond—all of it coalesced into a wall of impenetrable sameness. Sometimes I could hear Gwen in the next room, huffing in rhythm to some deep-knee-bends, some targeted core routine. Sometimes, particularly early in the morning, just nothing: hush of lake water pulled taut as a canvas; a dark, Hopper-like purple-blue, under a gray-blue sky.

And the biography, too: all miniscule font with (oddly) very few images. Most any reprieve from the relentless tediousness of documenting a rather tedious individual's life—even that of a striking painter like Hopper—came in small-scale drawings, in black-and-white reproductions of his lesser watercolors. No big, glossy, full-page paintings to ogle. (They were all tucked in the back.) No lonely creatures staring out from the windows of those pages. The biography, the puzzle—with its impenetrable gray-browns, dark blues, and near blacks amassed on our table—the lake outside, my life in isolation: all of it ponderous, seemingly meaningless.

Each evening early on, after completing a few dozen pieces of that first birds-and-oranges puzzle, I'd take my cheap kayak out on the lake with a beer and binoculars, snoop around the shores of the small, shaggy island for a green heron or some wood ducks, enjoy the simple pleasure of doing nothing. For a while I took photos over the nose of my kayak at sunset. "My office," I called it, and posted the proof online.

I quickly understood, though, that it was a dickish thing to do. Gwen and I got our groceries delivered, stayed the hell away from people, could afford to hunker down and not worry about much more than how to pass our days doing puzzles, reading about puzzling people, puzzling over their lives and our own, identifying the bright plumage of birds.

Once I stopped posting the kayak photos, though, I started approaching my isolation more morosely. It all felt somewhat illicit, the simple act of doing nothing and not fessing up to it, frittering away hours on a puzzle, while all around us reeled ominous reports of a death-dealing virus only the privileged could afford to avoid.

I peered out the windows at delivery trucks, waited for them to pull away before opening the door. I motioned to the guy at the taco stand to put the bag in the trunk. I let the phone ring and the email pile up. I drank more.

And just as Hopper returned again and again to nostalgia and old, fusty houses; and just as he detested anything that smacked of modernity, so too did I revert to looking at old family photos, texting my sister and brother various *do-you-remember* salvos: that pineapple-orange soda called Cactus Cooler; that kiddie, purple, banana-seated bike with streamers; the old, stone wall across the street from our house growing up, where we rummaged for snakes and scorpions and other dangerous things in the blinding gloss of southern California in the '80s.

And the Hopper canvas, too, evoked for me my own family dinners of chop suey: that vaguely pan-Asian (yet completely Americanized) dish featuring a congealed, gray slurry of corn starch and soy sauce, to which my mother would add canned water-chestnuts (super exotic) and mushrooms, before scooping it all over instant rice. Then, the moment of pure nostalgic reverence to me now: once tableside, we kids would dump crispy so-called Chow Mein noodles over it.

Such a classic American mashup: all our agglutinizing, all-in-one tendencies on show. And to be honest, I miss that. I miss those nights with my family now, my parents both dead, my brother and sister scattered across the country.

Hopper was no Rockwell, for sure. He was more like the photonegative of Rockwell, the underside of Rockwell, dark and malignant. Staring for hours at his *Chop Suey,* understanding intimately his abbreviated palette, his abhorrence of visible brush strokes (the Puritan in him erased most any marker of subjective passion), I was essentially training myself back into the past, my current life (job, friends, travel) shelved as neatly as board games, as puzzles in a linen closet.

No wonder, then, that I focused first on the scant color in the canvas: the flashy *Chop Suey* sign, of course, followed by the green of the main character's blouse, which Hopper echoed in the matching table lamps. (Frugal, staid, conservative Hopper.) But also the warm—it *is* warm, I can say that—sunlight flaring on the wide sill to the side of the women, spreading down the wall, lighting up that casually hung jacket. Truth is, the canvas is full of warmth, at least in terms of color.

And out the window, to the far right of the canvas (Hopper violently cropped his paintings after multiple sketches, recasting the subject from different angles, zooming in and out): is that a fire escape? a ladder descending to safety or ascending to the rooftop? Ladders almost always assume the work of symbols, of movement in either direction, of flux, of dynamism. Is this painting the puzzle I had thought it was, not for me but for Hopper? Was there, hidden among all that grainy blah of the darkened back walls and silence of that unhappy couple, was there at least a glint of hope? Was there—as that ladder implied, as the burnished walls and windowsill implied, as the women sitting there in that cheap chop-suey joint implied—a sneaking sense that things would get better?

Black Monday was right around the corner from the completion of this painting; so, no, things would not get better. But as for me, in 2020—as the COVID tallies leveled out and, in some places, dropped, as states started reopening—there was, it seemed, a sense that out of the isolation and grainy facsimiles of days, out of all that anxiety and fear might arise a new appreciation for what was most important to us.

I felt closer to Gwen, loved on our cats, wrote about my father, my mother, my friends—which is this book—relished the painterly play of that pinkish, maudlin sunlight over the water at dusk. I baked bread, trimmed the azaleas, started a garden, cared for things.

Then, out of the same-day everyday of our sheltered lives, videos surfaced of George Floyd, murdered by Minneapolis police, and the whole world was set ablaze again.

To finish the puzzle or not; to read a boring biography about the painter of a lost America; scenes that, already in the '20s and '30s, seemed anachronistic, elegiac, out of touch with modernity, and, let's face it, sad; to do any of that during mass protests against police brutality and racial injustice seemed, well, pointless at best, hopelessly wasteful at worst. Holed up in our house, Gwen and I dug deeper into our shared isolations. I slowed on the puzzle and the biography, both of which started to strike me as exercises of just the sort of privilege the protesters were rallying against: that we could sit there with our silly puzzle and budget rosé, bitching about the lack of baker's yeast through Instacart, while poorly paid people braved the grocery stores and FedEx lots for us, and delivered it right to our doorstep—cat food, paper towels, blueberries, all of it. Our brimming recycle bin—smashed boxes just about the color of Hopper's unburnished windowsill—was proof of our complicity.

"I don't know," a friend and fellow writer told me around then, as we discussed the protests and government crackdowns, "just feels like writing about my middle-aged white-lady problems is silly now." And so, too, my plague-year meditation on Hopper, even the Hopper painting, which—for all its angular grace and understated complexity, its balance of, and care for, those withdrawn colors—is itself an expression of privilege, nostalgia for his courtship of Jo: two young artists in their twenties, well off (and white) enough to occupy studios in Greenwich Village and play at the Bohemian life, to pass the anxiety of The Great Depression painting, building a vacation house in Maine, generally becoming wealthier.

And that restaurant, too, the chop-suey joint: in light of the protests against racial injustice, suddenly all that nostalgia seemed dubious, questionable. Such eateries—plentiful by the '20s—represented the last bastion for the mass of Chinese immigrants, who, in the long wake of the Exclusion Act of 1882, found themselves relegated to laundromats and restaurants. Immigrants who, for the most part, had no formal kitchen experience, quickly found a way to take their sense of food—what they had eaten back home but not necessarily prepared, what was by then more nostalgia than substance—and adapt it to a bland, Puritanical American palate repulsed by the fishy, the funky, and, by association, the unalloyed foreign.

Those self-styled cooks made do with whatever they could source (and their potential patrons could stomach). The term chop suey itself is merely an Anglicized iteration of the Cantonese *jup suei,* meaning *odds and ends:* inoffensive vegetables in something resembling Sunday gravy, all over rice: surely a dish their smug, privileged, white clientele might eat and enjoy yet still feel as if they had experienced the exotic, the *oriental,* the other. Soy sauce as the tolerable marker of foreignness.

Is the painting, then, also representative of institutionalized racism? There were tours, we know, at the turn of the century, which folks (white folks) could take of Chinatowns, ogling and tsk-tsking the brothels, opium dens, and chow-chows. Dark tourism, we call it now. Approached that way, the women in the painting—and the Hoppers, who also frequented such places—were part of that suspect privilege, fashionably Bohemian, getting dirty with the immigrants.

Hopper prized himself for the way in which his paintings rendered interior complexity suddenly manifest. "Great art," Hopper once remarked, "is the outward expression of an inner life in the artist." But what are the ways in which great art (perhaps unwittingly) also reveals the hidden values of an unjust system?

The end of the puzzle was a sea of muddy purples and sandy browns, the differences between the two subtle colors difficult to parse with the glare of the overhead light and my worsening vision.

"This is impossible," Gwen said one night, "and not much fun." And it wasn't.

By then, though, Gwen had taken up the challenge with me, putting in more time, now that the puzzle looked closer to completion. Or maybe she just wanted the thing gone. Regardless, sitting there, hovering over it, trial-and-erroring, one by one, each piece, gently chiding one another for mixing up the pieces we had already attempted: it was as close as we could come to turning off, taking a break from the COVID numbers (which were rising again) and the protests (which had not cooled down).

We were going to be there for a while, in the house, peering out at times at the lake rippled by crosswind, at times at a world we hardly knew existed beyond our driveway. We were like characters in a Hopper painting, for sure, completing a Hopper puzzle, whose subject was the puzzle of how we chose to spend our days. We could have been protesting in Atlanta. We could have volunteered to be contact tracers. We could have done lots of constructive things with our time, our seemingly infinite time. Instead we chose to stay put and sit and complete a puzzle, and reflect on those lonely women modeled on a lonely woman, painted by a lonely man.

Loneliness was our privilege, it seemed, isolation our choice. We had been living with that fact for almost three months. We would have to live with it much longer.

Aftermath

"I have really bad news," John texted me. "I won't be able to play the gig."

I was with my sister in Portland, on break from a writing conference, early in 2019, before my father died, before the plague descended. We sat at picnic tables outside the rolling, metal doors of a machine shop turned microbrew. My eighteen-year-old nephew Sam busied himself with a floppy-eared puppy at the table next to ours. The weather was glorious: crisp and clear, with that hollowed-out, northern sunlight raking the trees.

"After the cath procedure today," John wrote, "I was told to take it very easy until after open-heart surgery and its aftermath."

Open-heart surgery? my sister asked. Was I aware? First I'd heard of it, I said, a bit shocked, as I sipped my beer, a cloudy New England–style IPA, which left a metallic tinge on my tongue.

John was sixty-two and otherwise healthy. Didn't smoke, didn't drink excessively, ate sensibly, exercised. He and I traded smoothie recipes and swapped flax seed for cacao nibs. We ordered burgers and fries on occasion, too, but ran and biked and kayaked and generally cared about our health.

"Those surgeries now," my sister (a pharmacist) said consolingly, "they're like changing tires." She meant well, but I felt out of sorts, imagining John at home.

He and I, along with a few other friends, play in a kind of project band, we call it: we choose a group or album we all like, call up friends for any extra parts we can't handle (backup singers, keyboards, percussion, and horns), and twice a year play a gig at the local dive bar. We were slated for our next show, the entire Beatles *Let It Be* album, in a few weeks. We'd have to postpone. For a moment, I even felt disappointed. Then I felt guilty for feeling *that*. We couldn't do the gig without John. We wouldn't. And what did it matter anyway?

Mostly, though, I felt overly aware of my own chest, hyper-conscious of the weird muscle beating there. And that warehouse district in Portland, the industrial drill press on display inside the brewery's doors (a remnant, a vestige): it all made my sister's analogy for open-heart surgery—"like changing tires"—seem harsh and disembodied. I imagined the stacks of spent radials herringboned along the sidewall at the local shop back home, the smell of vulcanized rubber baking in the heat, the residual grime embedded in the hands of all the men who worked there. I didn't—I couldn't—imagine what John was poised to undergo.

"I'm scheduled for a consultation on Monday," his message continued, "and for surgery on April 10. Wish me luck!" Just like him, I thought, to mitigate the severity with a tag like that, as if he were trying to place in a local 5K or tackle a bathroom renovation.

More beer arrived: some citrusy affair with a big, floral nose. It was like drinking a box of marigolds.

"Don't worry," my sister said, as she took a sip. "Super common. He'll be fine."

A two-seater Mercedes stopped at the streetlight below us, a massive poodle in the passenger seat, romping back and forth in that tiny car. People around us giggled and pointed as the dog barked and carried on. When the car finally took off, I was relieved.

"He'll be fine," she repeated, and we sat for a moment watching Sam. He had by then made himself at home with the puppy next to us, roughhousing with it, down on his knees, on the concrete, his torso erect, in a kind of prayer position, it seemed, inviting the dog.

"Come here," he said, patting his own chest, "come to me, right here."

When I returned home a few days later, I asked John's wife, Muriel, how he was handling it all.

"You know John," she said. "Not one to show a lot of emotion."

And Muriel, too, I have to admit, seemed quite calm, eerily so. Perhaps a defense mechanism, perhaps a bit of John's stoic nature. Muriel and I are actually closer friends. We run together a few times a week, talk constantly of running (typical of runners), and gab about the university we teach at, she in the German program, me in English. I was in a unique position, it seemed, to notice their behavior but especially hers, which seemed markedly calm, measured, thoughtful, not given to excess or speculation.

Whatever the case, I humored it all, repeated what my sister said about how common the surgeries were (omitting the part about the tires). We had a longer run planned with some friends that next weekend. I asked if she'd join, what with John's surgery slated for earlier in the week. "Who knows?" she said. "Would like to."

Before going any further, I should say that the surgery was a success. Apart from the scar—which John didn't mind showing, exhibiting, like a battle wound or a marker of pride—and some residual pain in the "harvest areas"—leg and mammary veins removed and reapplied during the course of the surgery—he appeared and acted completely normal. Muriel said the nurses at the post-op checkup called him a model recovery, said they wanted to frame a photo of him for their wall.

But for the day or two after the surgery, for John as well as for Muriel (who sent me notably frightened messages), the whole thing was hardly easy, hardly common. The doctors had prepared them to expect some strangeness: that he'd swell ten pounds above his normal weight with the fluids pumped into him; that he'd initially feel cold and rubbery to the touch. Still she remained unprepared for the brutality of it, the immediacy, the irrevocable sense of trespass, the markers of it everywhere: the parting of the sternum but also incisions in the leg and groin, in the neck and chest, two tubes sent up through incisions in the belly and into the thoracic cavity to drain fluid.

I could tell she was shocked and horrified, but also just scared. Who wouldn't be?

A day after the surgery, in fact, John's pulse soared to 200, which, though not an uncommon response to the procedure, sent the room into a chorus of beeps and alarms, sent nurses into the room to manage it, sent Muriel who knows where: some green hell of helplessness and fear and anger at the precarious, ludicrous smallness of us all. It must have colored the world around her, too, around her husband, in that beeping room in the Emory Hospital ICU. Not only would John never be the same again; neither would she. In some ways I might even say that it changed her more, but that's probably stretching the facts.

All I know for sure is that I visited them the following Monday, after the hospital had released John. He sat in a recliner, acted and sounded fine, given the circumstances. He said the pain meds helped but that coughing hurt the most. The doctors had given him a special pillow—a red, heart-shaped pillow—which he was instructed to hold (embrace even, with his arms crossed around it) when a cough came on. I couldn't decide if the shape of the thing was ergonomic or overly cute or just plain insensitive.

It was my birthday, oddly enough, April fifteenth, and I felt self-conscious about the two of them telling me so, asking what I had planned, what Gwen and I were going to do, how I was, in short, going to celebrate. I didn't have much of an answer.

Muriel brought us beers; John was not allowed just yet. We ate chips and salsa from a small table between us. Their dog Toby, a tiny thing, got his head stuck inside the chip bag, and we all laughed, which felt terribly insignificant next to the scars and various bandages on John's body. He sat with both arms flat against the sides of his chair. The air was heavy; the conversation, consciously light; the seriousness under it all, palpable.

That day, in Paris, Notre Dame burned down.

Concentrations of sadness: they pool in unused bedrooms and attics, in musty warehouses never turned into microbrews, in the ruins of a Gothic church. They collect there, even well up. Or they seep into the floors, into our waking hours; darknesses and desperations unreal in our otherwise sunny everyday.

The day my mother died, for instance, after a quick decline—small hopes of improvement one by one cut away, dismantled—I remember how unreal it all felt. That could not actually *be* my mother. I knew that was not true, that the woman in that bed—with the tubes down her throat and the maze of IVs and monitors, the slow rise and fall of the sheet on her chest—I knew that was her. Still, to imagine the end as it really is—final, irreversible, and utterly complete—and to watch helplessly as a loved one enters its province: that's more than most of us can fathom. Even when dying is a kind of relief—an end to senseless suffering—even then, we need time to reframe the event, to structure it in a way that consoles rather than shocks, mitigates our pain rather than augmenting it.

I remember, too, at some point during her final hospital stay, my sister and I went out for lunch. It's all we could do to keep our minds occupied. She ordered a busy, Italian-style hoagie with lots of oil and pickled peppers, olives and such, cured meats and smelly cheese. When we returned to the hospital, my brother scrutinized her and took a sniff in her direction.

"What?" she said.

He smirked. "You smell like a sandwich."

Why do I remember that bit of levity in the face of my mother's final days? Why that and not some somber tangent playing out on the television in the waiting area, some fittingly wise bit of advice handed me by a wizened nurse in white scrubs, even my own reflection in the mirrors of the elevator interior? Why the absurdity and silliness of the stink of a sandwich?

On the internet, on my birthday, before John and Muriel's and the chips and salsa, I watched the tall spire of the Notre Dame cathedral wrapped in flames, the shaky cell footage capturing the moment it collapsed, imploded. "Unreal," friends posted.

News outlets ran it on the front page. Gwen texted me. "Have you seen this?" she asked. And of course I had. I sat at my desk and read all the reports coming in. Was it an act of terrorism? Was it because of the ongoing renovations? Did a mischievous crow tuck a still-lit cigarette into a nook in the spines of its roof? That last one I made up, but nobody knew for sure and so bandied about the wildest of speculations.

When the truth finally revealed itself—that, who knows?, it was just its time, the attic section seemingly made to catch fire, like dry kindling stacked and poised for the slightest of sparks—it did so unceremoniously. Smoke simply funneled off the top of that spidery mass of stone on the banks of the Seine. That's all. "It was bound to happen," I remember hearing a broadcaster suggest. Maintenance was shoddy anyway, the stone literally crumbling under the touch of a human hand; gargoyles, like tiny lepers, losing parts of their bodies here and there; Notre Dame itself—bits of it anyway, day by day—falling to the ground to be blown away, or swept up and dumped by the ceaseless city crews.

That eerie moment when fire simultaneously eats away the exterior and interior of a structure—a house, a tower, in this case a church—and we see the bones of the thing revealed, the metal or wooden skeleton against a backdrop of angry red and orange: unreal. But by *unreal* I probably mean an *excess* of the real. We grow accustomed—it seems obvious, I realize—to things as they are: a church, a friend, a mother, a world. We are in many respects such dumb animals, easily numbed by the normal. All it takes is some faulty wiring and a spark, a hereditary tendency toward plaque in the coronary arteries, the tiny mutation of a virus, and the unreal reveals itself: placid, unwrinkled, paradoxically young. Ponce de Leon's fountain was a nightmare he never woke from. The Cybil—wanting only to live forever—ended up wanting only death. Tragedy is eternally youthful.

Such dumb animals, yes, but lovable, like Toby with the chip bag on his head, like the poodle in that Mercedes or dopey puppy lunging, leaping at my nephew Sam, pawing at his chest, the owner looking on, smiling, in love with the dog, yes, but maybe in love, too, with that stupidly ideal afternoon in Portland, the sun piercing the canopy of that shady city street, scattering like coins on the pavement and the tops of passing cars. What did *we* care? *We* were not suffering.

☠

Just over a month had passed since John's surgery, and I was in Italy, as I had been each summer for the seven years prior, running the university program. I remember we took the students to Spoleto's duomo, which always elicits semi-muffled exclamations, mouths agape as they stare up at its façade. *Here's the church; here's the steeple.*

When we walked through the elaborate porch area and into the church itself, I watched as their eyes rose, taking in the vaulted nave, the bright (almost unreal) frescoes above the altar, all the height and richness of the place. The grand churches of Europe do that to us, causing our heads to tilt. They make us feel small, intentionally so; they almost force us to consider our own insignificance. I don't need a church to do that anymore. Besides, I don't find the interior that fascinating anyway. The frescoes, sure, but the rest is whitewash; the rest is bargain baroque, epiphany on the cheap.

The floor, however, is another story, with its fastidious geometry of muted greens and reds, triangular tesserae of Egyptian and Greek porphyry breaking and reforming in swirls and fitful cycles, large white stones bordering them, trying to contain them, imparting a semblance of order; stones softened and polished by the feet of the penitent, the dull finish of them—I know it sounds odd—almost organic, biological. It's as if the entire system were alive, and in some sense it is.

Daniela, our tour guide, explained to the students that in studying that busy Cosmatesque pattern on the floor of the nave, we could understand the dimensions of the original church, which was irrevocably altered over its history, enlarged by Pope Urban VIII, partly destroyed by the 1703 earthquake, metamorphosing, expanding. The church has become larger, yes, but also strangely plainer, a kind of reverse-engineered opacity in which the present grows ever foggier, while the past remains exquisitely detailed, complicated, alive.

Foggy present, complex past: that is not just in the church; it's in us, too. Such dumb animals, we mill about in our own self-important schedules, tunneling into computer screens and books, fixated on what's in front us, time-stamps deactivated, surroundings blurred. That day in Portland, as I sat with my sister and thought about John, the world suddenly enlarged. I was shocked out of my natural complacency, at least my desire to feel no pain.

"It's like losing a member of one's family," said an onlooker, as Notre Dame trembled in the heat of its own immolation. All the witnesses, in fact, lining the streets, observing the horror from a distance: what kept them rapt by the destruction if not the unreal beauty, the revelation of it all? *Open the doors; see all the people.*

Meanwhile the smoke rose in heavy, cylindrical, swirling masses dividing the air between them, over the placid rows of townhomes and prim, stately edifices along the river, in the Île de la Cité, the island where Paris began and where Notre Dame—at least the version we have known—ceased to be what it was, the beating heart of the French Republic.

Of course I know that the church will be rebuilt, may even prove somehow better for it, made less prone to fire, bereft now, I suppose, of what experts referred to as "the forest": a hidden network of hoary wooden beams and trellises in the attic of the structure; a Dantean dark wood of desiccated lumber, of potentiality, waiting to ignite. And I know that John, too, is better for the surgery, as if he had a choice. "The first symptom of heart trouble," a friend told me in the days after John's surgery, "the first symptom is often death."

Or maybe it's the simple fact of coming out the other side that is reason alone to celebrate, even without improvement. Maybe having your sternum sawed down the middle and split open with clamps, maybe that's revelation enough. *Open the doors.* Maybe it's the movement through, the crossing of the threshold.

That church floor in Spoleto is nothing but a record, a history. Like John's scar, it's a reference point, a marker of persistence, a reason to continue.

Somewhere in my house lies a photo album of my backpacking trip with Vince through Europe. Twenty-three and self-styled worldly, we bunked in flophouses and cheap hotels, ate mostly one meal a day. In

Paris, we stayed in a ratty hostel that served cheap beer and gave us access to a kitchen, where we—in surely one of Europe's culinary centers—ate canned ravioli and potato chips. *What an opportunity blown,* I think to myself now.

We did not, however, skimp on churches and museums, arches and towers. In that photo album, yellowing and blurred, is a photo—I can almost form it in my mind—of Notre Dame. Gray sky, I remember. Vince and I are not in the photo. Just a rather off-centered, amateur, tourist shot of the thing, squat and Gothic.

And yet a kind of relic status surrounds that photo for me now. Back before digital cameras, I could not know what awaited me on the film. (It came in rolls then, which adds another layer of antiquity.) I just pointed and clicked and waited and hoped. I carried around rolls of undeveloped film in my backpack for a summer. I worried I would lose them or that they'd be contaminated, that the entire trip—the record of my having been there among the towering histories of Europe, monumental and polished—would not exist. The unreality of Vince and me, the two of us having broken the bonds of complacency that kept the rest of our friends gathered—as if around a warm, inviting fire—in that small, southern California town we grew up in; the unreality of our adventure rendered real, attested to, verified and acknowledged not by our experience and our memory but by flimsy, corruptible, transparent film, a substance so fragile even exposure to light proves fatal.

In that Portland warehouse district, after the second beer, after reading John's message, I watched my nephew Sam with that puppy. Sam has had his problems, too, and a spate of surgeries as a result of his premature birth: malformed ear canals, scoliosis. The smile on his face, though, and complete abandon with which he addressed that puppy in all its wired, uncontainable joy: that pleased me, yes, but also blended with the news from John to create something close to the way the sunlight—pleasant but aggressive and angular—the way it found and warmed us through the tree-lined street.

That warehouse district full of microbreweries and boutiques, tattoo parlors and rigorously researched cocktail lounges—locales trying desperately to appear both within and without tradition, immersed and yet afloat atop the currents of history—proved, in hindsight, not just where I was (where I will always be) when I heard the news about John, but—I think now—where I *had* to be. I would not (*could* not) have experienced John's news otherwise, nor taken that odd joy in watching Sam roughhouse with the puppy, down on all fours himself, completely given over to the ritual of play, to the way we had all—my sister, Sam, and I—turned that machine-shop-microbrew into a church, at least the chapel John's somber message had rendered it.

When I went to pay, when I walked inside, past the antique drill press on display like a relic, over the concrete floors and around to the bar, where a few regulars hunched over their pints, the brims of their baseball hats pulled down low, obscuring their faces, as I waited for the bartender to return, I considered how the music—some metal song rumbling below us, persistently vibrating the floor with its bass—mixed with the few people chatting, the low ruckus of the kitchen crew in back—how it all blended in that cavernous interior, echoed off the polished floors, reverberating in the exposed ductwork and girders, the high rafters above, creating what I can only recall now as a hush, almost meditative, almost spiritual, most definitely memorable, now that I have remembered it.

Homecoming

At the court of the Phaeacians, a concert by the minstrel Demodocus. This is the age of heroes, of myth, and the blind bard sings of just that: a quarrel between Odysseus and Achilles. With a taut-stringed harp in his hands, Demodocus performs with such skill and pathos that the court's guest—a wanderer recently happened upon them—subtly draws his mantle down, concealing his tears.

Whatever we say of the ancient Greeks, they were—at least from what we glean from scenes like this—not much for crying. And yet cry they often did, if mostly in secret. Men (heroes, even) cry over lost lands and distant kingdoms, their forebears gone, their palaces in disarray. Even Odysseus, that most heroic among them, sheds tears for his beloved home on Ithaca and for his family there, if indeed he still has a home, if his family still lives.

The texts are certain of this stance on crying, particularly *The Odyssey,* in which this episode with Demodocus appears. And that guest at the court of the Phaeacians, the one who pulls the heavy hood over his face to hide his anguish: that is Odysseus himself, recently washed ashore; that is the hero, listening to a song about himself, about who he once was.

In the official concert video for "Unchained," Eddie Van Halen, shirtless, wears only the classic, winged "VH" necklace, white chinos, and knee-high candy-cane socks. Half the time the camera catches him—this is early footage, part of the age of heroes, of *guitar* heroes—he is all smiles, aping for the fans, both those visible in the arena and those beyond the lens. The rest of the time, his eyes appear closed, in some distant kingdom of memory, blind choreography, and joy.

And it is joy, in fact, that he embodies, at least in my recollection, the perfect expression of it, dwarfed by those Marshall stacks behind him; and by Alex, his brother, enthroned amid a massive drum set on risers. Beyond the speakers and drums, beyond the gong—which, during the end of the song and video, Alex will light with fire and bang—beyond all that, a cityscape backdrop, lights panning over the two-dimensional citadel, out to the massive arena crowd, all those hands in the air.

Catching one of the live Van Halen videos on MTV when I was young, in the heyday of the network, was like happening upon a spit of land after tossing about at sea. There amid the seemingly endless new-wave concept videos, which usually featured retro-stylized, '50s-era big-government fears and Cold War trench coats on foggy riverbanks; amid the hokey editing—not yet an art, not yet recognized or even understood, a foreign idiom—in videos by Styx or Scandal; amid all that, this raw, sweaty, human performance erupted, and I would sit rapt, on orange shag carpet, in front of the big console television.

The year must have been '81 or '82, the footage from around then, too. (The band released *Fair Warning*, the album on which "Unchained" appears, in 1981.) The sensation I have of recalling it, though, which is the same sensation I have when I watch it now, in the year of our Lord 2021, is of a time much greater, infinitely more expansive. It's as if I inhabit that room again, with its shag and wood paneling; I enlarge the present, dilate it, inject that past into it, Van Halen as a kind of bellows. The particular year of the video's making is, finally, irrelevant. It is, for better or worse, in all honesty, a rendering of my adolescence, part of the soundtrack of whatever I call my youth, however poorly I spent it.

I know I am not alone, though. In the comments underneath the video on YouTube, any number of versions of me have chimed in, all with various shades of nostalgia and hagiography.

"I want to meet the people who do not love this," one fan writes, "and just study their ability to not be physically assaulted by me." Or another: "If you can't get excited from this, you are a corpse."

that song came to rest in the fossil bed of my adolescence. Listening to the song now is like shearing away at a cliff side in South Dakota, the mandible of a man-eater coming into sharp relief.

Maybe *that's* what Odysseus cries for: not who he was but who he could never be again, the home not so much out of reach but rather out of time.

"Tell him your story, Gary," my mother said one night at the dinner table. Must have been '85 or so.

My father looked at me and smiled, finished whatever bit of food he was working on and wiped his mouth.

"At the tire shop today," he said, "a guy sitting next to me in the waiting room asked all about my car." My father took meticulous care of his 1957 Chevy, a car he let me take to my homecoming, and in which I could not play Van Halen. (No tape deck; just AM radio, to this day, hand to God.)

My father then recounted how this burly guy with a bushy beard, in a pair of jeans and a black t-shirt, how he asked all the right questions—how long had my father owned the car (since 1960), what size engine (283), what sort of shifting ("three on the tree")—in short, the kind of shibboleths that attest to and verify a man's enrollment not just in the club of classic-car owners but in the club of men, the ownership of one's own masculinity.

He told my father that he, too, had once owned a similar car, a '56 (never as good in my mind, slightly less alluring, abbreviated, unfinished, caught in a molting stage), and that he lamented having sold it.

I may have invented that last detail, since I heard countless versions of it while driving around with my father. Any gas station or convenience mart, any grocery-store parking lot became a kind of regal court, in which my father held the scepter and various men came to kiss his ring, rue the passing of their own versions of his car and, by extension, former versions of themselves. "Ubi sunt," the Latin poets said, "qui ante nos fuerunt?" "Where have they gone, those who came before us?"

or, to put it another way—the way The Kinks framed the question, in a song that Van Halen covered (*Diver Down*, 1982)—"Where have all the good times gone?"

That's the end of the story, though, really. My father said the fellow was quite amiable, that they sat there and chatted while the mechanics lowered the other guy's car—a Porsche—back to the world, gave him some paperwork to sign in the office.

And when the guy left my father in the small waiting room (black coffee in white cups, car mags with crusty edges stacked uneven on a side table) and entered the Vulcan-like forge of the shop proper, with its grime and men with their names in patches like tattoos on their chests (all this emphasis on being, on individuality, on attribution), with a boom box for all I know blasting Van Halen (something early, a deep cut), the clerk looked at my father, then out the office window to the shop again.

"Do you know who that was," he said to my father, "the guy you were just talking to?"

Oblivious as usual to celebrity of any kind, my father simply knitted his brow (I like to *think* he did anyway; this is my epic to tell), jutted his lower lip out like he did, and replied that, no, he didn't, that he had no earthly idea.

"That was Michael Anthony," the clerk said. "The bass player for Van Halen."

Certain Van Halen songs allow for two simultaneous auditory events. In one, I am my former self in the early '80s; in the other, I am the person listening in his home, some forty years later. Take "Romeo's Delight," particularly the coda, in which Roth repeats, "feel my heartbeat," while the band builds behind him: I am again driving my ludicrous, midnight-blue 1968 Camaro up Benson Avenue, stereo rattling the seats, as I take the curve into 21st Avenue, in Upland, California. (That small town with its nifty name, its aspirationally urban and orderly thoroughfares.) The silvery leaves of olive groves shimmer in the windshield, and the world seems receptive, nurturing, alive with my own sense of dominion over it.

"Running with the Devil": that song plays forever low in the bed-room of my friend Kirk, late at night, his parents sleeping in the room next door with the television on. (Westerns; always Westerns.) We stare at the lone, red LED on his boom box and imagine the power of those instruments the band wields with such *sprezzatura,* a word I surely didn't know then but which I understood perfectly, intuitively. Such *sprezzatura,* such artful nonchalance.

Or "Dirty Movies" in Tony's El Camino, windows down, driving to the beach. Or Tom and I singing, belting out (out of tune, of course, but in our minds idealized versions of ourselves) the silly, almost Vaudevil-lian mayhem of the lyrics to "Ice Cream Man" or "Happy Trails" or any number of Van Halen half-jokes, recorded because they could, because they were that good, that lovable, that powerful. I remember them all, *remember* in the deeper etymological valence of that verb. I am recon-structing those moments, re-*membering* them, those auditory halluci-nations once more made whole.

Reconstructions, though, are often painful. I swear I can feel the excruciating moth-weight of Eddie's guitar pick in my right hand (even though I'm a lefty), the equal and opposite reaction of Alex's stick hit-ting that dampened drumhead. (Nobody else played with such a dead snare—that sound of primitivism, of animal skin or of animals *being* skinned.) I swear I feel it all, the way a war hero feels a ghostly limb, feels its ache as loss, or its loss *as* ache: air-guitaring as a form of stretch-ing the muscles of my atrophied past, a not wholly unpleasant pain.

That's not quite right. I don't feel those sensations again as much as I feel the distance between *that* me and the person writing about it now.

Sometimes—even for the crude, outdated, predictably sexist, stupid lyrics and programmatic structure of a Van Halen song—I am moved, not so much by the music but rather by the lack of it, by the absence of that song over the past twenty, thirty, even forty years, and by the painful recognition of this fact: time has passed.

I am moved, yes, but by my own volition. I have done the moving. I have traveled out of that innocent, ignorant, childish, childhood realm. I have left my home.

Rituals of dispossession mark us: toys neglected then banished to a spare bedroom closet, finally given en masse to other people's kids or dumped on the loading dock of a Salvation Army; those tragically unfashionable bell-bottoms or Members Only jackets purged from the wardrobe, and with them the bonds that tied us to former iterations of ourselves. We are pupa in that regard, maturing through acts of metamorphoses and castings off, the soft shedding of previous versions, shells of ourselves.

Or take my old collection of CDs and my periodic culling of them, the attempts to portray a certain sensibility, a habit of mind, an intellect, simply through the ordered spines of jewel cases. Was it fate, testament to some more objective assessment of the group's ultimate power, or just plain obstinacy that made me never want to sell those Van Halen CDs? Something in me, even as I willfully, gleefully traded in hair metal for bossa nova, classic rock for classic jazz, something in me could not part with *Van Halen I* and *II, Women and Children First, Diver Down.* I can picture them all now, can even reimagine where I was when I first saw their covers.

Vince could freehand the vignettes of the *Fair Warning* album design. I adored the iconic simplicity of *Diver Down.* (Only much later did I realize that it was just a Scuba flag.) I remember how my cassette version of *Van Halen II* bleached over time, the tape losing its higher frequencies, muddying. (We might hold onto cassettes for the value of their physical form, not for their capacity to preserve.) These are relics to me now, meaningless to most but for me still carrying nostalgic charge.

I am not proud of my enduring love (can I call it that?) for Van Halen. Hardly. I am embarrassed by my juvenile adherence to these artifacts, let alone to the audio hallucinations they engender. I am embarrassed by who I was when I first listened to those songs, who I am again (always, sort of) when I hear them.

It's not Van Halen's fault that I was stupid and careless and somewhat dangerous to myself, gunning that silly car of mine around Upland like a fake hoodlum, fake bad boy with a busboy job, blasting bad music out the windows. Not Van Halen's fault that I *did,* as their song encouraged, take my whiskey home one fateful night, and drink too much of it while jamming with friends in the garage, my parents out to dinner.

Okay, maybe Van Halen *was* a little at fault there, since "Take Your Whiskey Home" (seventh track, *Fair Warning*) instructed me to get "halfway to the label" before I might "even make it through the night." Surely not Van Halen's fault—how could they have known?—that my erstwhile uncle, a man I never knew, a man who died in prison (phony checks and scams galore), was an alcoholic, and that my teen drinking, as stupid and posture-obsessed as it was—rekindled those memories in my mother, who laid into me the next day, crying over a different species of nostalgia.

Not Van Halen's fault that I idolized them, wanted to be some amalgamation of them all: the flamboyant, big-circus acrobatics; the deft handwork; the sheer machinery of the band. They were an enterprise, a culture, an economy, but even more than that. They were—for better or worse—the roundest, fullest expression of the joy of being who I was and the suppression of all that I never thought I'd end up being. They were the tidy embodiment of a raft of emotions—the finest I could fathom—in the mythic world of adolescence I navigated.

The cover design of Stanley Lombardo's translation of *The Odyssey* features that famously stark, black-and-white print of planet Earth, seen from the surface of the Moon. William Anders snapped it on December 24, 1968, while part of the Apollo 8 mission. What a gorgeous visual analog to the sense of desperate exile that Homer's epic tries to capture, the overwhelming pain of removal.

True, to the astronauts on that mission, Earth (their home) was mere hours away, even if the distances were great. Odysseus, on the other hand, was absent twenty years. We know that mythic fact before we even crack open Homer's text, or at least we learn it very quickly: ten years of warfare, ten years lost at sea, amid all manner of sorceresses, nymphs, ogres, lotus eaters, cannibals, and the like.

That image, though, that tiny swirling marble cast into thick ink—with the slightest bit of the Moon present for scale—that image is *The Odyssey* encapsulated. All Odysseus wants is simply to go home, and yet.

At times, in fact, home is right in front of him; he just can't get there or doesn't know where he is in relation to it. Looking at any map of Odysseus's purported voyage (at least as charted by Homer), we see instantly the great lengths he has been forced to travel, the distances he suffered: from the shores of Ithaca, to the Trojan citadel, to what is now Africa, Sicily, and beyond. We see them, but we remain—because of the confines of the frontispiece map—geographically restricted, the Mediterranean framed and cropped.

The truth of it is this: Odysseus didn't really go that far at all. Modern cruise ships manage something similar in no more than a week. And with piña coladas.

When Vince and I backpacked across Europe all those years ago—we, who, in unguarded moments (by then also self-proclaimed music aficionados) probably still listened to Van Halen—we thought we saw a serviceable chunk of the world. England, France, Netherlands, Germany; the shores of Liguria, the monuments of Rome, Florence's crowded opulence. We experienced Greece (ate McDonald's in Athens), even Turkey, Austria, the Czech Republic. For nearly two months, my friend and I crossed the continent, eating strange foods, meeting strange people, visiting strange lands. We were little Odysseuses, especially when we returned, since we brought that expanded sense of the possible, along with our own slightly haughty vision of who we were, masters of European transit and money, brought all that home, a place then hardly large enough to contain us.

And maybe *that's* what home is, what coming home signifies: that the place can no longer afford to have us there.

I can still draw, with reasonable fidelity, the classic "VH" logo. Like the wings of a majestic eagle, its twin letters soar over the memory of my teenage years. Or they resemble sails, part of a larger vessel bearing me beyond the threshold of the '70s and into the '80s, where the nautical metaphors of popular music continued to suggest that sailing away, that escape in some seafaring form, was not only desirable but possible. But escape from what, exactly? And why?

I can still draw the logo, and I am not alone. Here, then, is a brief and incomplete corpus of answers I gathered from friends, when asked if they, too, if called upon, could freehand those signature Van Halen initials:

Yep
Yes
I'm going to say yes
Without a doubt
Absolutely
Easily
Blindfolded
With my left hand
Abso-fucking-lutely
On every notebook I ever owned from 1982–1985

Odysseus, too, if called upon, at ten or fifteen or twenty years' distance, in the very cave of Polyphemus, or skirting the vortex of Charybdis, could have probably sketched with reasonable fidelity the contours of Ithaca. His kingdom, at least the version in his memory, was immutable, immaculate. So, too, is my kingdom, the realm I access through Van Halen songs, the citadel of adolescence. "Childhood," a friend of mine wrote, "is the country we all come from and to which we can never return." We are all, in other words, exiles. It's just that some of us never realize it.

A particularly poignant moment occurs late in The Odyssey, when the hero finally reveals his true identity to his son Telemachus, who—a young man by then—could have barely recognized his father, gone twenty years. Though it takes some convincing, finally the son realizes that this stranger, who was just moments before, as Van Halen might have put it, "broken down and dirty, dressed in rags" ("Dead or Alive"; *Van Halen II*), this beggar in disguise is his father. Odysseus has come home, Telemachus. "Salt tears," Homer writes, "from the wells of longing in both men."

Here again, more crying.

What's more, their shared tears engender a curious simile. "Cries," the bard continues, "burst from both as keen and fluttering as those of the great taloned hawk, whose nestlings farmers take before they fly." Their tears, it seems, form two divergent types: those shed in joy at reunion and those testifying to the loss of some twenty years and, with them, the absence of an entire relationship.

Odysseus's son is no longer a child. The hero never knew Telemachus as a "nestling." His son was, in a metaphorical sense, stolen from him. Odysseus has missed the sum total of his own son's growth, and Telemachus his father's presence. The tears are salt indeed, since there is no way for us to distinguish which sort of tears they are. (Salt, after all, is painful in a wound but essential as well. Its sting also purifies.)

"So helplessly they cried," Homer writes, "and might have gone on weeping so till sundown." But what then? Are they simply wasting more time in eulogizing the time already wasted? Or is it that the pain of recollection and the joy of homecoming are essentially identical? Is there just *one* sort of tear shed here?

We are all exiles, yes, and, by remembering our exile, more beautiful—at least more human—because of it.

What, then, to make of my own father, whose musical canon fossilized in the late '50s, who seemed caught in a kind of audio amber, forever asking me with near-breathless excitement, when a particular song came on the radio, if I had heard it before.

"Yes, Dad," I would say, "a hundred times."

"Theme from *A Summer Place*," "Rock Around the Clock," "Pink Shoelaces," pretty much any song by Elvis prior to 1960: these and many others constituted the soundtrack to my father's perpetual adolescence and teenage years. I want to know what it felt like to him when he heard Sam Cooke or Otis Redding again, driving his '57 Chevy. I want to know if there was any shock from the distance irrevocably revealed not ahead of him, on the actual road, but metaphorically behind him, in a nearly irretrievable past.

My sense is that there was no shock, just a continuum. Those were the same songs he had loved for most of his life, playing out of the same radio, the same speakers, the same car; the same tunes compressed and filtered through transistors, part of the very air he breathed.

He was an Odysseus who stayed home, who passed on the great voyage. He never set sail. His kingdom remained intact.

The story of Van Halen—and here I mean the brothers—was also one of epic travel: from the shores not of some mythic land but from Amsterdam, whence their Dutch father (a musician himself, a clarinetist) and Javanese mother took the boys and a piano by boat to the New World; to Pasadena, California, not far from where I grew up, where my father was born and raised.

In the Smithsonian interview with Eddie, he spoke of that voyage, of having been exiles themselves, he and his brother, of playing piano on the ship between his father's sets (performing to pay for his family's passage); of the later ascendancy of Van Halen as a group, in the waning days of disco and punk, in Los Angeles; and of the tinkering Eddie did to guitars, carving holes out of his Fender Stratocaster to accommodate the Humbucker pickups from a Les Paul; of all the innovations rendered that much more impressive by the fact that this legend, this guitar hero could not read music, never could. Like Homer, he was blind.

And strangely musicless, if I don't count his childhood immersed in the tunes of his father: big band repertoires and wedding polkas, played at gigs in which both Eddie and Alex were at times part of their father's backup band. In the Smithsonian interview, Eddie said that he idolized Eric Clapton (as Odysseus idolized Achilles, I like to think: one hero's admiration of another) but only while Clapton played for Cream. Once he went solo, Eddie said, his interest waned, and not just for Clapton. The last album Eddie bought, so he claimed, was Peter Gabriel's *So* (1986). After that, he could not say.

Eddie, I might argue, lived metaphorically blind *and* deaf, in an auditory realm of his own making. What was nostalgic, would *could* have been, for him? What music summoned tears? My bet would be one of his father's tunes: the warm, round sound of a clarinet, the human resonance of a reed on the tongue.

I say that because at the end of the Smithsonian interview, during the Q&A, when a guy with a Van Halen shirt (the VH in a kind of mock alloy) asked Eddie about all the dead musicians who came before him: of all of them, whom would he choose to play with again? Eddie stared into (and past) the small audience in the auditorium, so much smaller than the arenas to which he had by then become accustomed; stared into it, past it, took just a moment.

"Wow," he said, "I'd love to jam with my father again."

Sing to me, Muse, of that man skilled in all ways of commuting, the father in his vintage car, who braved Baseline at rush hour, who exited the 210 Freeway four exits early to snake and wind amid the subdivisions of West Covina, to avoid the worst of the honking and the backup, to labor finally in a distant kingdom. Many taillights home he endured, blurring the edges of sleep and boredom, abiding the hawk's-eye traffic reports from Bruce Wayne—KFI's "Eye in the Sky"—enthroned in helicopter, trolling above fleets, flotillas of cars awash in the Los Angeles basin.

He suffered his son's juvenile excess, the mock drag-race he lost his license for, the times he drove his father's car half-drunk and underage, under Helios, god of the sun, and the judge that blotted out his driving privileges, wanted to lock him up. But he could not save his son from his poor music taste, could not fathom why the windows of his bedroom and his own badass car rattled.

Launch out on his story, Muse, daughter of Zeus. Start where you will. Sing for our time, too, of this man of 500,000 miles, three engines, and just one car.

💀

Songs within songs. Songs, in some sense, *about* songs, self-referential but not wholly similar.

Sons who resemble their fathers, who emanate from their fathers; sons who, at times, are frightened by the likeness.

I wonder if Telemachus—whose own miniature epic comprises much of the first four books of *The Odyssey*—ever worried that he was doomed to follow his father's plotless journey, to be sucked down a watery hole or end up as a pile of forgotten bones picked over on a far shore, at the foot of some broken city wall.

I wonder if Eddie and Alex—growing up in Pasadena, getting bullied at school for their foreignness, sleeping with their parents in the same room, in a house with two other immigrant families—if they imagined for themselves a fate similar to their father's, a talented but largely luckless musician washing dishes and gigging on the weekends.

When Odysseus finally beholds his son, a man by then, aged twenty or so, twenty years have passed between them. Odysseus is, in some sense, looking at himself at the age at which he left Ithaca, barely a man, brave and dumb enough to follow some of his buddies out on the wine-dark sea, antiquity's answer to *the road:* the original, sold-out, world tour.

I wonder if every Van Halen song—though the lyrics, critically and hopelessly mannered, chronicle the usual debaucheries and mock freedoms of being young and stupid—I wonder if the songs essentially *had* to be about nothing. They were aggressively pointless in the way art often strives to be, repeating sexual metaphors the way Homer repeats his epithets: "grey-eyed Athena"; "feel your love tonight"; "cow-eyed Hera"; "baby, baby, baby"; "rosy-fingered you know what I like."

The song, it seems to me now, inside any Van Halen song, is one of continuity. Perhaps that's true of most any rock song: that it first and foremost references itself, reinforces the surprisingly strict set of invariable characteristics of rock-and-roll the way each home in the subdivisions that surrounded me growing up in California, the way each one reinforced the rest: each with a tidy lawn making the adjacent lawns glimmer, with timed sprinklers, a low wooden fence, the big bay doors of the garage concealing the hold, the past—ruptured bicycles and exposed ribs of patio umbrellas, the messy workbench with its menagerie of turpentine and caustics and foul-smelling emollients in coffee cans, the reels and reels of family footage yellowing in their metal shields.

This is true of most any rock song, perhaps, but is particularly poignant with Van Halen, whose lyrics, whose nifty, doo-wop background harmonies, whose shuffles and big-band-era showoffness never seemed wholly part of the contemporary soundscape anyway, and instead conjured an alternative past, the past in which the Van Halen boys' father with his clarinet, the boys with their piano on the boat, all of it kept shifting back and forth, from verse to chorus to solo to coda.

What does Odysseus weep for, really, when he hears Demodocus sing? It's complicated, I know, but so is the machinery of nostalgia. We don't choose our own brands. We don't order it readymade, though it arrives intact and instantly deployable. A certain Van Halen song plays, and already I see the past unload its cargo, its *nostalgia* (Greek for *home pain*) into me. I come face to face with who I was all those years ago. I have traveled back, I have returned, the song tells me, and I am surprised to find myself once again on the shores of my old kingdom.

And when Odysseus boards the Phaeacian ship bound for Ithaca at last, the ship loaded with gifts from King Alcinous and his court, gray-eyed Athena casts the hero into a deep sleep, so deep in fact that upon arrival he slumbers still. And after the crew has gently laid the hero and his treasures safely upon the shores of his own island; after they have set out again across the sea; when Odysseus wakes, home at last, he doesn't even recognize where he is. The final irony of Homer's epic of homecoming is that the hero can't even celebrate it properly. He simply thinks he's landed on another strange shore.

Then again, *that* Ithaca—the one stabilized in his memory, inert, calcified twenty years prior—*that* Ithaca is gone, and in its place this replica in which a model of his manor stands but is instead populated by rowdy suitors, rival bands, rocking all night long; where Odysseus's great father Laertes, once king, has taken himself away to the hills, overcome as he is with grief for his missing son.

No wonder Odysseus doesn't initially recognize his home; in some respects, it no longer is.

And then I think of my own father, how—though no musician—he would wave his pointed index fingers in arcs toward one another and back away, as he imagined an orchestra conductor would do, when one of his favorite oldies played on the radio, and he would interrupt me and turn up the volume, ask if I knew the song, if I had heard it, which I always had, a hundred times.

I think of my father, as Odysseus does his, cast into the hills with his olives and sadness; as Telemachus does his, gigging out on the wide Mediterranean, tearing the house down; as Eddie thought of his father, all of them now gone, part of memory and music, the song within a Van Halen song, which, when I hear it, makes me think of my own father, born in the year of our Lord, 1941, in the kingdom of Pasadena, state of California.

Unsent Letter to the Living #4

Dear XXXXX,

That my brother, sister, and I did not have the stomach to sell off the contents of our father's house should be quite obvious. My brother, though he lives closest, treated the house like a small Chernobyl, his brief missions into the tragedy always tightly timed and monitored. My sister and I were even worse, almost physically ill just thinking about the place, poking hesitantly in the cupboards and back closets of our memories. When we convened in the house after our father's death, we remained careful not to dislodge some torrent of sentiment, some unforeseen ache suddenly in the heft of a particular quilt, the scent of baby clothes in a cedar chest, the burnished red of a toy car from our father's childhood.

The weight of the thing, I said to her, was disarming—curiously heavy, elemental.

And that we possessed little in the way of motivation to seek intermediaries (you purveyors of the dispossessed, you brokers of grief) should also come as no surprise. Left on the shores of that new land—an island without our father on it—all we could do was set up shop, learn the idiosyncrasies, where to place our feet, what news from the outside world. We had to figure out how to survive, and part of survival, I suppose, meant entrusting others, forming alliances with folks beyond our tribe.

Yet how to know the hostile from the human, the devil from the do-gooder?

So when my brother said that the realtor with whom he had worked years ago, that she had recommended you and your estate-sale company, my sister and I said, "Sure, let's go with them": that, too, should come as no surprise. And though the name of your company—Dusty Gold Estate Sales—gave us pause (death and grief not being territories predisposed to cuteness or providence or treasure), still we were weak and lost. We huddled on the shore. We warmed our hands around the fires made by the stories we told, tales of the time before the wreck. We wondered aloud to the stars how it was our own bodies worked, by what mechanisms they continued to draw water and air and food and joy.

We made interminable lists. We signed forms. We relinquished keys. We drank straight from the bottle.

What *was* surprising—after your crew had begun its grim work of parceling, inventorying, and pricing—was the smell of the house, the scent, the stench. Yes, you had already begun your work when we held vigil in the house over a long weekend, just, as my sister reasoned, "to be together there, one last time." We had flown in for a few days "for closure," she said. The house, though, seemed to have opened some wound, had begun to disintegrate itself, malfunction, its body cancerous, succumbing to processes similar to those that led to our father's death.

We imagined a dead rat in the crawl space, dead possum caught in an attic vent, dead squirrel in the makeshift mausoleum of a wall. Dead anything, dead something. We winced through the clutter of closets, opened gingerly those upstairs doors. Dead silence.

Instead it was a clogged toilet, which your workers left for us, and which I found with a skin of paper towels thrown hastily around its base, a water line having spread like some terrible nimbus onto the carpeted anteroom.

All weekend in that foul-smelling house, a few weeks after our father's death, we suffered greatly, suffered that smell, too—that curiously human, rotten, damp-towel, organic nastiness, along with the chemical cover-ups of your cleaners in dubiously Caribbean casts. We kept the smell as constant companion, reminder of our weakness and knee-jerk need to cover up our pain.

Fitting, we thought, that we smelled what we were living in: a morass; a sludgy, odorous, odious pit of responsibilities laced with regrets; a house full of not much any one of us could handle or store or bear to part with.

We had reached the outer limits of our lives together, the border of what held us in place, the edge of a fetid pit.

In Dante's *Inferno*, when the poet and his guide reach the very depths of the chasm and behold Satan himself half-buried in ice, flapping his enormous wings across that frozen expanse, we as readers are poised for a riveting, diabolical speech from the instrument of ultimate sin, our inheritance from a Manichean myth that imagines the world built of some epic struggle between the forces of good and evil. We have come to think of Lucifer as a near match to God's greatness; some Bizarro-Superman of sorts, a twisted, backward "S" on his chest; an all-powerful worker of the dark, libidinous, and chthonic (I love that word), his smell animal and repellent, his feet cloven, his breath a foul, chemical cocktail.

Instead, what Dante offers us is a giant, pathetic, mute loser. Cast down into deepest Hell, Satan can only contemplate his sorrowful state—torn from God's side for eternity, banished to that sub-zero wasteland—and so does what we mostly did that weekend, in our own version of exile: he cries. Satan cries, and down the hairy, matted, discolored, pitiful, pit-thrown jaws of the monster run whatever passes for tears.

Your crew (and whoever clogged the toilet) merely made a metaphor from bodily waste and effluvia: we were down; we were mired in our sadness; our existence rotten, seemingly irredeemable. You were there to help, you might say, and this rough justice of yours was perhaps for our own good. It forced us to realize our harsh predicament, that we'd have to forge through that underworld if we were going to survive in this new land.

No Yankee Candle optimism; no Febreze to mask our feverish doldrums; no sanitizer strong enough; no damn potpourri.

It occurs to me now that anyone who frequents estate sales is nothing more than an insect on fallen fruit; one of many locusts who darken the late harvest sky; a dung-beetle; at least part of the chorus of the damned who wail forever in the bowels of Dante's foul-smelling metaphor for the worst, most self-centered, narcissistic, predatory assholes among us.

And those who enable, pander to, harbor, even abet these vectors of despair and detritus: well, you can probably guess.

Maybe I just want to look away. Maybe I like the questions Dante seems to pose about morality, even as he levies his invented tortures (premeditated and exquisitely ironized) on his own worst enemies. Surely I admire the imagination it all took, not to mention the math, the numerology, the command of various spiritual traditions. Still it took a friend of mine, a Medieval scholar of the Bayeux Tapestry (that long scroll of war and propaganda), a friend more attuned to the evils people are capable of, to reveal to me what I had not seen before in the structure of Dante's hell: that despite all of its complexities and elaborate metaphorical machinery, it's just a big shitter, a place for excrement to go.

And there at its deepest reaches, down at the drain, clogging up all the works, is the foul-smelling, slimy brown, pathetic piece of shit himself, which you forced us to confront in all his steamy ordure.

Fun fact: *potpourri* comes from seventeenth-century French, and means *rotten pot.* Do with that what you will.

"If you're going through Hell," Winston Churchill once declared, "keep going." And we, too, were at war, battling armies of ghosts, who were in turn led by mercenaries like you, professional profiteers, lieutenants of the lost. But who are we to talk? We hired you, after all.

And we did make it out the other side, if just barely. We washed ashore with our guilt and meager artifacts from that former dynasty, our lost Arcadia.

We sold the house, finally, by then just a shell, a carapace. It's been over a year now since I set foot in there, but it is my hope that every last remnant of your trespass is cleansed, and that the first thing one encounters now is the smell, Lethe-like, of forgetfulness, which is—regretfully—not one I am familiar with.

Sincerely,
Chad

The Best Kiss Story Ever

"A thought experiment," Vince said, "involving Kiss."

January by then, almost a year into the pandemic, when the poor weather and general malaise had forced most of us to huddle inside and stew. I searched for diversion as keenly as a hawk scours farmland. But Kiss?

"Not what I had in mind," I said, even though I could already feel my tongue writhing to some faint, demonic rhythm.

The backstory: in the late '70s, as Vince reminded me, the four members of Kiss—most likely coked up and burned out on each other's runny makeup and post-concert solvents—did something audacious. (And this is Kiss, mind you. Audaciousness—at least whatever kitschy subgenre they trafficked in—was kind of their thing.) Instead of releasing *one* album, one Kiss album to follow the eight previous (all recorded in four years, which is—let me do the math—a blistering two albums per year), they released *four* albums, four *solo* albums, one by each member, all on the same day: September 18, 1978.

"Now admittedly," he continued, "these are not great albums."

"Amen," I said.

Even correcting for the fact that we were speaking of Kiss—famous for such songs as "Love Gun" ("You pulled the trigger of my [. . .]"), "Rock and Roll All Nite" [*sic*], and "Dr. Love"—*great,* as a modifier, seemed already on shaky foundations.

Yet what if they had only released *one* album? Could we—my friend mused—construct a hypothetical compilation of, say, ten songs, culled from those four mediocre efforts?

My first question, frankly, was not *Could we?* but *Why would we?*

"You don't mean that," Vince said.

It's true: I was once fond of Kiss. He and I both were. In late '70s southern California, any semi-rebellious boy (with nothing substantive against which to rebel) probably was. For a brief run, I was even a card-carrying member of The Kiss Army, though what sorts of obligations and privileges such affiliation entailed lie beyond memory now.

"You might be surprised," Vince said. Turns out—as he started to listen to those albums again—he found better-than-listenable songs, decent hooks, even some tight musicianship. Turns out that certain Kiss members, unchained (pun intended) from the getups and hangups and record-label expectations—managed to express some modicum of individuality, what lay beyond the grease paint and platform boots.

In doing so, Paul, Gene, Ace, and Peter engaged in what I might even call a sort of tacit arms race, enlisting heavyweight musicians and hired guns, featuring voguish-diva cameos, trying to one-up their band-mates. Gene Simmons, for example (at the time dating Cher), boasted contributions by Joe Perry (Aerosmith), Rick Nielsen (Cheap Trick), Jeff "Skunk" Baxter (Steely Dan), not to mention Helen Reddy (hand to God), Bob Seger, and (I shit you not) Donna Summer. Rumor has it he nearly bagged Lennon and McCartney on a song or two.

What the hell, I thought. I had the time. Plus the albums were mercifully brief. I could listen to them on my morning runs, be done in no time, and do right by my friend.

Besides, I also admit to some curiosity. What would those albums sound like to me, more than forty years later? Could I access again that part of my life? Would it matter?

"You can almost *hear* the cocaine," Vince added.

We begin with what we know.

Thinking that Paul Stanley's effort would establish a kind of benchmark—he fronted the band and wrote many of their most popular songs—I started there. Immediately the shlock hit me: hackneyed lyrics (watered-down Kiss fare) and a brittle, almost tinny sonic texture made me question why I had ever liked Kiss writ large, let alone Paul Stanley.

"Well?" Gwen asked when I returned from my run.

I chucked my earbuds and beanie in the bin beside the door.

"Kiss," I said, "without the blood and pyrotechnics."

"Meaning?"

I looked at our cat licking himself on the kitchen floor.

"Worse than Kiss," I said. "Diet Kiss."

Which was not completely fair of me. Nervous and uptight anyway, sent back into the classroom in the middle of a post-holiday spike in COVID cases, I worried about everything, including how much I worried. I sat in the university parking lot later that morning, engine idling, a parenthetical-heavy, pandemic-prescient (or so it seemed) Paul Stanley number playing—"Take Me Away (Together as One)"—and fretted over my small class, my scared students, and my '70s glam-rock challenge.

I was frustrated, too: at the school, which mandated in-class instruction and slashed our staff lines; at the students, who were not to blame and probably frustrated themselves; at that goddamn mask, which itched my nose and fogged my glasses.

I began retro-sympathizing with Kiss and their face paint: the clogged pores, the rashes and chafing.

I scurried inside, taught as best I could, then bolted for the door. I Googled the recommended duration in a closed space with others, wondered about the school's ventilation system, frowned through my mask at the long-empty hand-sanitizing station near the building's entrance.

Everything seemed empty. Empty and pointless and simultaneously threatening.

On the other hand, the few students who showed up for class acted—at least behind their masks—genuinely interested or just relieved by the respite a writing class offered. We grew, in my mind, quickly fond of each other, starting our class periods catching up, swapping stories.

"Tell me," I asked them later that week, "something embarrassing you did when you were young, but which, now, you are okay with."

"I wore Spiderman underwear to school" one student said, "until I was, like, nine."

Another student spoke of once catching an older brother watching porn and then watching it with him. When I asked why she thought she did that, what was going on in her head, she looked pensive (at least what I could tell through the mask).

"I grew up," she said, "in a house full of boys, five brothers."

The other students by then were riveted, all looking at her.

"I guess I finally felt like part of their club."

And since I would not ask of them anything I would not ask of myself, I shared with them my own story.

"When I was young," I said, "I loved listening to Kiss."

I owned a small Panasonic cassette player, red with a black handle, black buttons, almost Kiss-like itself in its loudness and brazenness and (then) space-age sleekness. I don't remember how I acquired the machine (birthday present? hand-me-down?), but popping in Kiss's *Destroyer* (1976) or *Alive* (1978)—cassettes I must have pilfered from my older sister—felt both dangerous and empowering. "Shout It Out Loud," "God of Thunder," "Hotter than Hell": to a scrawny, pasty-skinned, freckly eight-year-old, those songs offered a nearly forbidden elixir of fortitude and freedom.

Did I understand the lyrics, the sexual innuendos, the rock-and-roll tropes? Of course not. The aural totality of Kiss, however, shot into me like a sharp shock, an injection. I hardly knew what I was taking in, but I knew it felt slightly illegal and really good.

An inoculation of sorts, but against what? A shield for my insecurities, but how?

I didn't sign up for organized football (was too afraid), could manage only soccer ("everyone plays"). Even then I wasn't very good. Lily-white, clumsy with a baseball mitt, fearful of bike jumps, I was introspective and gangly and preferred my *Star Wars* figurines.

Kiss: they were my immunizing agent. If not the cure, those four glam rockers at least provided protection against whatever common, unexceptional horrors plague a middle-class boy's mind: embarrassment in school, nerdy pastimes and accelerated courses, a fumble at recess, simply wearing the wrong goddamn jacket.

Or maybe Kiss allowed me some provisional membership into the club of older boys I admired, access to a shared vocabulary with David Justice, for example: neighbor and small-time badass who brandished bee-bee guns (absolutely verboten in my house) and let me shoot them (what?), who kept porn mags in a shoebox in the ivy and cypress between our houses, who owned (I shit you not) a pet alligator.

Or maybe Kiss was like *being kissed,* in the sense that I heard him speak of that dreamy phenomenon; of girls in general, who simultaneously represented poison (cooties) and cure (love). Listening to Kiss with David Justice—who dipped tobacco, for Christ sakes, who jetted around on an obnoxious, street-illegal dirt bike—was like carrying my own pre-pubescent Rod of Asclepius.

I was invincible with Kiss. I *was* kissed. I could—so I imagined, if called upon—rock and roll all nite.

A few weeks into the semester, having made my way through Paul Stanley, finding just one paltry song ("Ain't Quite Right") for my hypothetical album, and feeling the pressure, I progressed to Gene Simmons. Since the only Kiss solo tune I even remembered, "Radioactive," had issued from Gene, I figured—I *hoped*—he could save me.

Turns out that song, the album's lead (and presumably a harbinger of what awaited me), was terrible. The Vaseline-smeared lens of my nostalgia again proved inaccurate. Yes, I distinctly remember sitting on what my sister and I called our parents' "safari couch"—a pied, jungle-themed, velour-like sectional, whose coloring resembled rainbow sherbet—

listening to the album, poring over its liner notes all those years ago. In February 2021, however, it brought no recognizable joy, no recognition at all. Overproduced and underimagined, the song was shockingly tedious. Despite its fantastical, cinematic opening and Joe Perry's serviceable guitar solo, "Radioactive" remained typical rock schmaltz.

Vince, however, was unmoved, frustrated with my projecting unfair expectations onto poor Gene.

"You can't view Kiss," he said, "through 2021 glasses."

By then, though, I viewed everything—my job, my life, and not just Kiss—through the pandemic. My vision had grown as myopic as my patterns of movement. Sure, I was jogging, exercising a great deal (just about every day), but somewhat manically, in circles, around our small lake, listening to crappy solo albums by Kiss. "You look like a prisoner," a friend of mine joked on a run, referring to my weight loss. "Eat a goddamn cheeseburger, already."

And it's true, too, that I was eating less (stomach in knots) and drinking more, which, when coupled with my home-styled haircuts and spotty shaving, contributed to my gaunt, slightly wan, burned-out shtick.

Gene, to be fair, didn't help with "Radioactive," or the following tune, "Burning Up with Fever," neither of which offered much counterargument to anxieties regarding pathogens and sickness. *Screw this,* I said to myself by the spillway. I gave up and went back to a podcast about doomsday housing fads, folks living in renovated missile silos and the like.

How was I supposed to forget about where I was, anyway? What had happened to the world, when even crappy solo albums by a crappy band from the '70s could resituate me in dire danger and viral hysteria?

And then, as if on cue: a new release, the long-awaited-for blockbuster.

"COVID vaccinations" was the title of the email a colleague sent to me, a clutch of other department friends copied on it, a link to some site in Alabama.

"You have to register," she wrote (almost breathlessly, I imagined), "but they're taking educators."

In hindsight, of course, it was I who was breathless.

She said I'd have to keep refreshing the page but that it would only last a few minutes. I linked, registered, and started refreshing. Where *was* this place, anyway? *What* was it? At that point, I would have taken a derelict car wash or defunct Del Taco in the farthest corner of that state or any other. All I knew was that I desperately wanted the vaccine, wanted to stop worrying, stop fretting and stewing, stop drinking so much, stop listening to Kiss.

On my sixth or seventh try, a day's worth of times in half-hour blocks appeared. I took the one slot open—2:30 p.m. in two days' time—almost in disbelief. I checked my inbox. Bang. There it was: my name, officially scheduled. I checked the address: Auburn, about an hour and a half away.

I was booked. I was going to a Detroit Rock City in my mind.

"Get up / Everybody's gonna move their feet."

I called Gwen, then at work at the university.

"You'll never guess," I said, "what I just got."

She logged right on and—bang—an appointment the day after me.

"Get down / Everybody's gonna leave their seat."

Vince was right, turns out. The next day on my run, I returned to Gene and immediately hit "See You Tonite" [*sic*], a curiously Beatles-esque pop tune with slick harmonies and a big hook.

Holy shit, I remember thinking, as I ran by a gaggle of hissing Canada Geese by the boat launch. *Did I just find a listenable song?*

By the end of that short run, in fact, I had identified no fewer than three other Simmons compositions—"Always Near You (Nowhere to Hide)," which could have fooled me as a latter-day Beck acoustic number, "Man of 1,000 Faces" (O the irony!), and "Mr. Make Believe" (ditto!).

"I told you," Vince said that night.

We were each drinking a chewy Cabernet, decent but not exaggerated, as I rhapsodized about the harmonies, the surprise, the general (if still shocking) pleasantness of Gene's tunes, so far from the blood-and-fire-spitting bat-demon thing he played on stage.

"I told you," he repeated.

And he was right. I was hooked. I had the fever.

I wonder, though, how much my impending immunization colored my view of those songs. Was I merely projecting onto Gene some newly found Panglossian optimism? Weren't those 2021 glasses, too, if of a more inviting tint? Had I been, in some odd way, reinoculated *by* or *against* Kiss? Had I begun already to feel the effects of Kiss antibodies? Was the end to this plague nigh?

All I knew is that, driving down to that Auburn clinic the next day, listening to Ace Frehley—his album, the third in my story, my Kiss story—the thought of soon receiving the COVID vaccine, after that year of worry and mourning and teeth grinding and anxiety drinking, felt slightly illegal and really good.

A student asked to meet with me virtually, wanted to apologize for not being in class the last week. (Working two jobs, he said.) When I logged in and he popped up on my monitor, I paused. He did not look like the student I thought I was meeting.

"Yeah," he said, "and you don't look like the teacher."

He was right, I suppose. Without the masks, the COVID getups, we seemed almost naked. He expressed interest in going next in the work-shop, and we chatted about how his journal entries were progressing. The experience of seeing him, though, really *seeing* his face—the mechanism of his jaw, his expressive smile—and hearing his voice without the treble stripped away by layers of cloth: it felt liberating, as if I had been granted access backstage, could simply hang out with the band, no barriers, no cosmetics, no bouncers or security detail.

The simple thrill of seeing another human, up close, with no mask, a human I had spent considerable time with: that, too, felt slightly illegal and really good.

It occurred to me then to ask *all* of the students to follow suit, to set up some time with me online just to chat.

"Your call," I said, "what we talk about. Carte blanche."

Funny, though, as I embarked on my tour, seeing each of the students up close, noting the nose- and lip-rings, adjusting to the facts of their facial features under those masks, I realized the tour was more about me. I was the one in need of seeing them and not so much vice versa.

They were the group I wanted to know. They were the young, hip, make-up-clad band, and I was the groupie after my fix.

☻

Ace Frehley's album—the best-selling of the four (to Paul's and Gene's chagrin, I should think)—also proved the best *sounding* in the mix: a monstrous low end and kick pedal that thumped like a trash truck, screaming solos and a plush layer of distorted rhythm guitars that, in some vaguely Seattleite way, bordered on proto-grunge, especially when paired with Ace's odd time signatures.

"Rip It Out," "Snowblind," "Ozone," "Wiped-Out": Ace was just feeding tasty guitar licks into a hit-making machine.

Sure, the lyrics were awful; and his singing, terrible. Most tracks, however, rose above the morass of '70s hard-rock filler I had come to equate with the worst parts of Kiss.

Ace—at least the Ace reintroduced to me through these solo songs— reminded me of how my Old-English professor in grad school once spoke of Beowulf.

"Don't you have the sense," he asked us in class one evening, "that Beowulf is somehow *too good* for those he rescues, that they don't *deserve* him?"

Again, though, how much merit Ace really *deserved* and how much I could instead chalk up to my ever-increasing hope for humanity—the pestilence finally seeming to relent—I could not say. I had entered a new phase in my relationship with both Kiss and COVID. I felt free to enjoy what had felt slightly illegal just days before. I felt enlarged, capacious, able to retroactively provide for Ace's fledgling (if somewhat doomed) solo project, for my students and their shitty fast-food jobs, for Vince, my friend—my childhood, California friend—whose Kiss story was *my* story, too, after all.

I wanted to spread the gospel, told *everyone* about the Kiss challenge.

"Ugh," one friend wrote back. "They're abominable."

"You don't mean that," I responded.

I sent the link for the Alabama clinic, too, to anyone I could and then responded to their texts:

"Is it true?" and "They allow Georgia residents?" and "Are you fucking serious?"

Yes, yes, and *yes!*

Yes to the woman—I swear she smiled through her mask—as she prepared my dose, asked me—as I rocked uncontrollably in that cheap, plastic chair—if I was nervous.

"No," I said through that goddamn mask, "excited!"

"Shock me, make me feel better!"

Give it to me: more vaccine, more Kiss.

Yes to the off-duty security guard roaming the lot of us scattered in a holding area post-vaccine, ensuring that we were taking well to it, that we were fine.

"They call me Dr. Love."

Yes to Ace on the drive home, and to Vince as I called him, told him about the injection, how it felt to listen once more to Ace's songs: the slurry of bass and drums hardening into a foundation on which to situate the fuzz of those guitars; even the shitty lyrics—is there such a thing as a *single* entendre?—all post-vaccine, windows down in my mind.

And it didn't matter that "Snowblind" (one of my favorite Ace tunes) again seemed strangely prophetic of some viral-induced existential quandary. ("Am I ever gonna get to where I'm gonna go home / Maybe tomorrow, maybe next summer.") No, I cleaved more closely, in my newly immunized status, to the sentiment expressed in "Ozone":

"I'm feelin' fine, I'm feelin' good all of the time."

Thin lines on a hotel mirror, post-concert, somewhere in middle America. Thin lines, too, between evocative, boundary-challenging, flamboyant yet working-class Detroit bands from the '70s (The Stooges, for example, or MC5), and shock-and-shlock rockers like Kiss and Alice Cooper.

No matter. As a kid I knew only of Kiss, really. I lived a rather typical (if preposterously privileged) childhood, where Kiss (and its foot soldiers, like David Justice) represented the only minor contagion in otherwise vacuum-sealed safety and comfort. Iggy Pop et al. were simply strains not endemic to my conservative, southern-California enclave. Danger, thus, remained lurid, desirable, clad in leather and spikes, but also performative and, by design, innocuous.

Which is partly why, late in high school, I went as Gene Simmons to a Halloween party: cheap chains sourced from the garage, draped in an X across my chest and then around my waist; studiously torn jeans; whatever I wore as a shirt (ripped white tee? faux leather vest?); a store-bought wig with a bun on top of my head.

My mother giggled as she painted my face.

"Hold still," she said, enjoying the prank maybe as much as I did.

Because Kiss, at that point, was kitsch twice removed, double-layered schmaltz. To dress as Gene—along with my friend Tom (as Paul)—was to cloak myself in a commercial version of irony, which, at that age, in the late '80s, was not yet something my body manufactured on its own.

"Kiss!" people yelled across the crowded house, through smoke, raising their red Solo cups of beer. We were the hit, the stars, or so we thought.

Yet when the police showed up and people bolted out side doors and back exits, I remember sprinting down the sidewalk of an adjacent street toward my car, the stupid chains around my waist slipping down my legs, until they snared my ankles, catching one boot on the other, laying me out parallel to the cement full stride, such that—for one brief moment—I was part bat, taken to the air, a suburban Beelzebub.

Real blood out of the mouth, then. Actual torn clothes. Blood on them, too. Ragged chain links gouging my skin. Blood everywhere.

"Are you okay?" a few fellow partiers asked, as they huddled in their car with the lights out.

I was fine, unfortunately. Just embarrassed by my clumsiness and costume and dipshit, party life, which in some ways mirrored that of Kiss, if lighter on the cocaine. Working at a stupid restaurant, playing in bands in my late-teen years of partying and acting idiotically, my demon-bat flight reminded me of my own oblivion, aggressively brought me back to Earth.

As did a car down the street here, just a few weeks ago, after my first Pfizer shot, as I walked back to my house after a run, again feeling invincible. For I was finishing Peter Criss's album—the final of the four, the end to my story—which had proved by far the worst. ("Holy shit," I remember my brother texting me, after he too had begun the challenge, "This Peter Criss album is terrible!")

I had, though, endured most of Criss's anemic R&B efforts on that run and had grudgingly chosen "I'm Gonna Love You" for my compilation. (At least one song, Vince demanded, from each of the four.) A bit winded from it all—the run, the shitty songs—I absentmindedly scrolled through his titles on my phone, reliving the pain.

Oblivion, again? Smug contentment? The fact that I had not only survived my friend's Kiss challenge but had somehow thrived? That my body now harbored within it protean protection against a death-dealing virus?

And why had I chosen a different route that day, which meant I finished my preset distance leaving a half-mile walk at the end? What compelled me to walk, too, without looking to the left, ignoring that steep driveway, down which—and within inches of me—a dark SUV shot out backward, coming within a hair's breadth—a demon hair's breadth?—of Detroit-Rock-Citying me?

"Oh my God, no time to turn / I got to laugh 'cause I know I'm gonna die. / Why?"

Inches, I swear. Hand to God of Thunder.

Too shocked, too consumed with my own non-memories of what *could* have occurred, I looked back, inside the truck. I could not see the driver well, obscured as he remained through tinted glass and my own imagined horror. All I knew is that he seemed as shocked as I felt, and that—for whatever reason—I sensed a kindred spirit there, some poor creature as startled at what had almost transpired as I was.

"Here it comes again," Criss sang, "'Cause lightnin' only blinds my eyes."

I spent the rest of the walk home embarrassed at my Peter-Criss-instilled trance, my warped sense of invincibility from COVID, when all it would take was a driver not looking and a runner (having run) smugly peering into his phone, at Kiss.

And to my students, for whom I had given every bit of leeway, suspended my attendance policy, generally just labored to embody a friend, a confidante, as they navigated an all-but-irradiated campus, shitty jobs, and existentially dubious paths toward what may very well appear—in the glaring light of COVID—questionable degrees: I regret somewhat my Pollyannish antics post-first Pfizer shot, my pep talks to them to stay the course, to keep going through hell.

Not sure, in hindsight, I had many options. Act as if nothing or everything was happening, all at once: those appeared the two drastic measures by which I could continue to arrive and provide—what was it, exactly?—instruction, coaching, inspiration, or just simply an ear.

To their credit (or perhaps their weariness with regard to well-intentioned folks like me trying to pal up to them), they mostly just did what they needed to do, what the class called for. I couldn't tell, in what looked like then the failing light of a finally receding pandemic, just what, precisely, my students walked away with each day: a sense of purpose in the face of difficulty? A belief in the right to tell their stories, no matter how mundane or ignored or seemingly pointless?

"No story," I told them, "is pointless, so long as you know how to tell it."

I suppose if they left with just that—considering the pandemic, the virus, the odd, post-apocalyptic campus we walked—I'd be content. Plus, their stories of working shitty jobs and managing professors who played at benevolence, who channeled everything onto Zoom ("I *loathe* online courses," a student told me) or just simply ignored the pandemic swirl-ing around them in the shuttered storefronts of American normality—their stories were not much different than mine, my Kiss story: the absur-dity, the nostalgia for better times, the desire to enjoy a friend's company, to do something because it felt slightly illegal and really good.

☻

We end with provisional beginnings to other stories. We conclude often with what commences a complementary narrative.

Which is why, when the knock came at my door a week later—in my waiting for my next shot; in the middle of that odd, dystopian, pandemic semester; in what I thought was the twilight of COVID—I almost did not answer.

Who the hell, in that masked-up, circumspect world of virus be-lievers and deniers, who the hell went door to door? And who the hell answered?

A roofer, he explained, as he backed away from the porch. Said he noticed some damage and would I mind if he climbed up and took a look?

"Absolutely no commitment," he said, but if he could prove some storm wear, he would file the insurance claim for me.

"A good chance you could have a new roof," he said, "and only pay your deductible."

What the hell, I thought.

Later, after he was done, as he was taking my name down, he paused.

"I feel really bad," he said, "but I see you running all the time around here, and I almost killed you last week."

I would have never recognized him in that sobering midday sun (though he did resemble, at least in my mind, Peter Criss). Still, he copped to that near-manslaughter charge with no provocation from me. He self-unmasked, and that seemed noble, part of this better world in which I had begun to live.

I told him that I was just as much at fault, not paying attention, preoccupied with my goddamn phone. (I left out exactly whom I was listening to, omitted *that* part of the story.)

"Well," he said, "we can share the blame then and be glad nothing happened."

And yet, in my mind, *everything* had happened and *continued* to happen: my students just plugging along, resilient, weary but also prone to laugh and enjoy themselves in the ruins; my good fortune with the vaccine and the gospel of the vaccine in general; my Kiss story and that of my friend Vince, and the story we share together, which we relived through those less-than-great songs; my near-death experience and the roofer who revealed himself as the thankfully hapless Bat-Demon of Destruction and Woe that he was.

So when I mentioned to another friend, Ryan, later that week that I was nearing the end of my Kiss story and inching closer and closer to a fully-vaccinated status, I didn't care that he was a good fifteen years younger than I, that he might not even understand the layers of irony I had wrapped around that core of pre-adolescent truth. I didn't care that he might not comprehend all the ways in which I had labored to protect that vulnerable part of my childhood, yet how I wished in some odd way now—in my inter-vaccine state—to celebrate it.

"Are you kidding me?" Ryan said. "I have the best Kiss story ever."

The year 1975 was a great one for the Vikings.

Scratch that.

Imagine your grandmother in 1975, in a photo with Paul, Gene, Ace, and Peter in full garb. Imagine the five of them, then, not in some arena in Detroit post-concert but rather at Cadillac High School.

Scratch that, too.

How to retell Ryan's "best Kiss story ever," whose story it really isn't his to tell, let alone mine?

We begin with what we know.

The Cadillac High Vikings (which itself could be a Kiss epithet), 0–2 to start the '74 season, were feeling down when then-assistant-coach Jim Neff started to play Kiss in the locker room to loosen his players up.

Kiss—also a well-known acronym for a successful football strategy (*Keep It Simple, Stupid*)—proved in many ways the correct soundtrack for the team. And the Vikings did keep it simple, winning every game after that abysmal start. So grateful, at season's close, was coach Neff that he wrote to Paul, Gene, Ace, and Peter to relay to them the successes his team had enjoyed with Kiss as theme music. The band, to his amazement, responded, and there was found the kernel of another Kiss story.

There are Kiss stories *within* Kiss stories.

Would they—Kiss—would they consider playing the Cadillac High homecoming in 1975? Would they—now touring the world, from Tokyo to Los Angeles, "the hottest band in the world"—would they come to little Cadillac, seat of Wexford County, Michigan?

Yes to that invitation (I shit you not). *Yes*, too, to the homecoming parade (Hand to God of Thunder and Rock and Roll), in which Kiss participated, riding a float, everyone—not just the band—donning the makeup, the getups: little kids, grandparents, shopkeepers and managers, their faces painted like aliens, like bat demons, like cats, like . . . whatever a Star Child is.

Yes to that packed gymnasium, where Kiss (*Kiss,* for Christ sakes!) played for the students of a small high school, in a town whose entire population represented a fraction of a typical Kiss concert.

Yes to the civic breakfast the next morning, at which the Cadillac mayor, the superintendent of schools, the principal, and others, ate pancakes (pancakes!) with Kiss, all of them—the band and administrators, even the mayor's wife—decked out in Kiss makeup, which the band applied themselves during a chatty session beforehand, everybody in white smocks and big smiles.

Yes to the photo of Gene and the mayor—Gene in his hell-spawn leather, the mayor in his tweed suit—both in the classic, winged, bat-demon makeup, tongues out, aping for the camera.

And *yes* to the photo (which Ryan swears exists) of Ryan's grandmother (then the librarian and senior adviser at Cadillac High School) with the four members of Kiss, about whom, when Ryan asked her, she said were a nice bunch of boys, and very tall.

Scratch that.

Scratch it like an itch.

Scratch through that story, yes, and there are Kiss stories underneath: the fact, for example, that the members of Kiss still speak of their Cadillac gig in hushed, reverent tones.

"We were there for *you*," Gene remembers of the Viking football players, in a recent, online clip. "We were paying homage to *you*."

And when it was over, Kiss strutted onto a packed stadium field, as a distant whir became increasingly audible. From out over Lake Cadillac, a massive helicopter (a helicopter, for Christ sakes!) arrived, touched down on that field, and—to the adoration of a healthy cross-section of students and townspeople, many of whom arrived with painted faces, so that the entire place seemed, as Gene put it, a "Planet Kiss"—the band jumped in, said goodbye, and (I shit you not) ascended like the rock stars they were, dumping leaflets out over the crowd, thousands of them, all of which said, simply, "Cadillac High—Kiss Loves You!"

"My grandmother totally partied with Kiss," my friend Ryan said. "*That's* the best Kiss story ever."

💀

And it is.

But it isn't.

Stories: they prove difficult to isolate, taxonomize, archive. Ryan's story, which is more his grandmother's and, even more, that of the football team of a small Michigan high school, a story of infinite regress: what sort of story would it be without my childhood friend's Kiss challenge, without COVID?

What would the silly story my student told of wearing Spiderman pajamas to school too late into his life, what would that mean if not for a pandemic against which we might all, I suspect, harbor a wish for some secret, special power, at least some talisman against an invisible threat? And what of the student catching her brother with porn, wanting merely to be part of the band, to belong? We all have our David Justices.

And Vince, my childhood friend, with this Kiss challenge; Vince, who looks more and more like his father each year, who would probably say the same of me, though my father is now gone, the two of us dependent on each other now perhaps more than ever: how would Vince's Kiss story resonate if not for the shuttered storefronts of our quarantined lives, which provided—between the start of the semester and my full inoculation, between the plague year and what followed—the walls off of which those Kiss solo songs reverberated?

How to separate *that* Kiss (shock of our adolescent years) from *this* Kiss (salve to our pandemic fears)? For while it is absurd to believe a goofy glam-rock band from the '70s could in any way affect the outcome of a twenty-first-century pandemic, it is even *more* absurd to believe that they couldn't.

Because on the way back from my second shot in Auburn—as the sun began to set, throwing an orange-red, Tequila-Sunrise, rainbow-sherbet light across the dashboard, as I listened to "King of the Night Time World"—from *Alive II* (1977)—I, too, felt somewhat regal, untouchable, finally beyond the grip of that goddamn virus, the only pain then the rather biting (if pleasant) nostalgia for my friend and those days of singing Kiss songs, imagining ourselves as part of the band, before he and I went solo, broke into our separate lives.

Protection, I suppose. Protection from the virus allowed me to frame my Kiss story, to see in other Kiss stories the same narrative of better times, kismet and happenstance, of just being in the right place at the right time or—in the case of my near death at the hands of the local roofer—*not* being there.

Such that when the workers came a week after that to tear the roof off our house and reinstall it all, lending to our humble, little ranch home another thirty-five years of protection, an inoculation of sorts against wind and hail and the decaying maple in our neighbor's yard—

as they tore off the old shingles and pitched them in arcs out over the carport and into the dumpster, and as those bits of roof banged on the metal bin in a percussive racket I'm sure my neighbors despised, my parents would have lamented, and Gwen complained about ("My God, when will that *end?*"), I thought again of Vince, my childhood friend, and of our long friendship, and of the four members of Kiss, singing in unison, over those preposterous drums, far out over Lake Cadillac and beyond:

"Loud, I wanna hear it loud / Right between the eyes."

Printed in the USA
CPSIA information can be obtained
at www.ICGtesting.com
CBHW032002010324
4865CB00004B/74